300 SANDWICHES

300

SANDWICHES

A Multilayered Love Story . . . With Recipes

STEPHANIE SMITH

Z
ZINC
INK

Zinc Ink
Ballantine Books
New York

Published in the United States by Zinc Ink, an imprint of Random House, a division of Penguin Random House LLC, New York.

BALLANTINE and the HOUSE colophon are registered trademarks of Penguin Random House LLC. ZINC INK is a trademark of David Zinczenko.

LIBRARY OF CONGRESS CATALOGING–IN–PUBLICATION DATA
Smith, Stephanie
300 sandwiches : a multilayered love story . . . with recipes/Stephanie Smith.
pages cm
ISBN 978-0-553-39160-2 (hardback)—ISBN 978-0-553-39161-9 (ebook)
1. Sandwiches.   2. Smith, Stephanie, 1978—Friends and associates.
3. Journalists—United States—Biography.
I. Title.   II. Title: Three-hundred Sandwiches.
TX818.S628 2015
641.81–dc23
2014046306
Printed in the United States of America on acid-free paper

www.ballantinebooks.com

246897531

First Edition

Book design by Diane Hobbing

For Mom, Dad, and E, with love

CONTENTS

INTRODUCTION

You know your relationship has gone viral when Matt Lauer calls to ask about it.

Okay, it was somebody who works with Matt Lauer. But he wanted us on the *Today* show the very next day to discuss 300 Sandwiches, my blog about a bet I made with E, my boyfriend: I'd make him the food, he'd supply a wedding ring—a mutually beneficial deal.

At 4:00 A.M., E and I packed up a cooler's worth of groceries and hopped in a car to Rockefeller Center. The *Today* show is located half a block from my offices at the *New York Post,* where I work as a gossip columnist. I walk by the set every day on the way to work but had never gone through the guest entrance until now.

We stepped into the elevator and were escorted to *Today*'s prep kitchen, where I went to work assembling my first sandwich with an entire staff of food stylists who would help me make it look more like art than lunch. I was so nervous that I accidentally tossed the on-set pepper and paprika from the kitchen shelves into the bag of food I'd brought. I stole the *Today* show's pepper! Does Giada de Laurentiis do that when she's on the show?

The lights were blinding above me. I started to sweat. I caught E's eye. *Can I do this?* I thought.

He jumped in and grabbed the knife from my hands, which were shaking as I sliced tomatoes. "You can do this." That was all I needed to hear.

At 8:00 A.M., I sat in the makeup chair and watched as a reporter from NBC's local newscast gave a teaser about my segment coming up in the next half hour. "Can three hundred sandwiches make a man propose? Meet a woman who's doing just that, on the next hour of *Today*."

I took my place on the stage. As I walked out, I saw that photos of sandwiches from my blog had been blown up and displayed on large screens behind the table displaying my creations. The producers miked me, and I looked over at E and smiled excitedly. "Can you believe this?" I mouthed to him.

Then a flurry of people—producers, runners, pages, publicists—came to introduce themselves. And, as soon as we went to commercial break, the show's hosts, Savannah Guthrie, Al Roker, Natalie Morales, and MATT LAUER (!) ran over to me. Hugging, kissing, "Hello! How are you? These sandwiches look good!"-ing.

I felt like I was watching all this on camera, outside myself. This couldn't be real. I wondered what my mother was thinking. And what was *E's* mother thinking?

We were live. Savannah introduced me as a reporter for the *New York Post* and the author of 300 Sandwiches. The segment started, and they walked through each of my sandwich offerings, carefully displayed for the camera by the show's stylist. "Are you really making sandwiches in pursuit of an engagement ring?" Savannah asked.

"Yes," I said, answering calmly, again, playing the role of the confident female chef I was most definitely not. And then Matt went for the kill: "Some people said this young lady is setting women back fifty years; she's becoming a Stepford wife. . . . How do you react?"

I told Matt that E does most of the cooking at home, and then hit him with the kicker. "If he wasn't the kind of guy that was worth one sandwich, I wouldn't be making three hundred sandwiches."

"So let's bring out Eric, here." E came from stage left and joined me on camera. "Eric, what's your favorite of all these?"

"The prime rib." I knew he'd say that.

"Now, let's get to the real question," Matt said, gearing up for the hardball. I knew it was coming. So did E—I'd warned him about this.

"When she hits number three hundred, will you get down on one knee and will you propose?"

In that split second, I thought back to all the sandwiches I had made so far—174—it seemed like an astronomical number, and I still had so many more to go. I'd accepted this challenge on a whim, an inside joke between my boyfriend and me while we progressed in our relationship from casual to committed. But was an engagement ring really worth all the outrage that was looming just past the *Today* studios? Were five minutes of fame worth being a whipping post for every feminist rant the Internet had to offer, and having the man I love reviled on an international level? Was it worth all those sandwiches, and what they represented?

I was about to find out.

PART ONE

Love at First Bite

ONE

My parents met over sandwiches.

Sporting an Afro and a black pantsuit, the 1975 version of my mother, Jeanette, walked into a White Castle on Main Street in Orange, New Jersey, for some post-clubbing eats. She immediately recognized the guy ahead of her in line. They'd grown up together, lived on the same block, gone swimming at the local park together. Art—the version who had yet to become my father—wore Coke-bottle glasses, a bell-bottom suit, and a mustache so thick you could do pull-ups off it.

"Art? Art Smith? Wow, it's been years!"

My father paused. "Hmmm," he said, thinking of his smoothest line: "I don't know the name, but anyone as fine as you, I *should* know her name."

"Jean," she told him. "Jean Brown?"

"Jean! Oh, wow! How have you been?"

As they waited for sliders (before sliders were a thing), they exchanged phone numbers and agreed to go out.

On their first date, my father picked my mother up at her house in a "loud, souped-up" red Dodge Charger.

"It was so loud that when he started the car, you shook in your seat," my mother has said.

Her friends Debbie and Pam were also at the house, and the three of them packed a roadie of Scotch in their purses before they went out.

My father took my mother and her two friends to dinner in Manhattan, double-parking the loud Charger. When they were finished, Dad took the friends home, and he and Jean drove around and talked.

"What would you say if I asked you to marry me?" Dad said.

"Will you give me everything I want?" answered my mom.

"I'll give you everything in my power."

"Sure, why not?" Mom said. He pulled up in front of my mom's house, dropped her off, and drove home.

"I thought he was just joking, or just saying that to get in my pants," Mom told me later. I asked Dad about proposing on the first date. He said, "I knew what I wanted."

When I moved to New York, I knew what I wanted: a job.

I was a child of the '80s and '90s, Chicago-raised—my folks moved there six years after their fateful meeting. I cheered for the Bulls and Bears, learned about pop culture and politics from MTV, and spent more time worrying about my next volleyball practice than about whether or not boys liked me. I had a *Cosby Show* upbringing, except that the Brooklyn brownstone was replaced by a two-story home in a subdivision in the mall suburbs of Chicago.

I wasn't a nerd, but I was a Goody Two-shoes who followed rules and listened to my parents and rode my bike, up and down the safe streets lined with station wagons and American-made sedans, until the street lights would come on.

My house was typical suburban living. And my parents were a happy co-parenting couple. My dad, no longer the player who met my mom, was a man of two worlds. During the week, he was Corporate Joe; he wore suits and carried a briefcase and commuted to downtown Chicago to his banking job. If he wasn't working in Chicago, he was flying every Monday morning to a different state for work and flying home on Friday night in time for dinner. We turned driving back and forth to the airport into quality family time, listening to talk radio in the mornings or Soul II Soul singing *"Back to life, back to reality"* on the extended remixed cassette single (it was the '90s, people), and telling Dad what he'd missed at home during the week on Friday nights.

When he arrived home, Corporate Joe transformed himself into Country Joe—trading his suit and briefcase for flannel shirts and Dockers and fishing poles or shotguns.

My father, who was in the United States Navy for four years before he kicked off his career, can best be described as woodsy. He hunted deer, elk, quail, pheasant, and whatever else ran wild in the upper half of the country. He fished regularly, and bought me my first fishing pole—one of those red stick poles with no reel—when I was four. We had a small cabin in Michigan, on a lake in an unincorporated small town outside of Kalamazoo, where he loved getting away to fish or hunt. His Jeep or Blazer or pickup truck was always full of fishing tackle, camouflage overalls, poles, and duck calls. He taught me to swim, to bait my own hooks and properly cast a reel, to drive a boat on the water and back up a trailer to pick up a boat at the dock.

One of his proudest moments was when I caught a twenty-pound catfish with that rod by bobbing the bait into the water near the dock. The fish was so large it almost pulled me in. Dad scrambled over to grab the pole and helped me pull up the writhing animal. "I got it! Hold on!" he screamed. Before Dad could reach for the net, the fish snapped my frail pole in half. He thrust his hand into the water to grab the fish with his bare hands, but it slipped away. "Wow, Stephie!" he said, out of breath. "That was a *big* fish! You almost had him!" To this day, he tells the story to friends as if I did.

My mother, Jeanette, was not a minivan type of mom—she drove a *Camaro*. A Z28 steel-gray Camaro. I don't remember many other moms picking their kids up from playgrounds in sports cars back then, but I will never forget her obsession with getting a T-top. She sat behind the wheel wearing aviator sunglasses and a wide smile, her fluffy black Farrah Fawcett hair blowing in the breeze, whipping around the streets of our subdivision on our way back home.

Jeanette ran the home like a boss. Mom believed she could be an equal partner in her marriage if she took care of the home while Dad was the breadwinner. That's what her generation did. She took pride in having a neat and orderly house, where the laundry was folded at all times, the carpet was freshly vacuumed, and something warm and filling was cooking in the kitchen. She made cookies for the school bake sales and was a member of the PTA. She packed for vacations a week in advance, always had a week's worth of groceries in the fridge, and never let her car have less than half a tank of gas in it. My mother was ready for anything.

But she also relished playtime, and she was a top member of the village bowling league. True story: My mother was recruited to join the team after she bowled a 260 during her very first outing. Twenty years later, we still stay up until 1:00 A.M. bowling on Nintendo Wii. "Still got it," she said once, as she beat me in the final frame.

Mom went all out for the holidays, putting up decorations and buying gifts. Anything I wanted, I got. Remember that Christmas of 1984, when people were looting toy stores across the country to buy their kids Cabbage Patch Dolls? Moms were fighting in parking lots to get their hands on those scrunch-faced dolls. And guess who got TWO for Christmas that year? This girl!

Mom went back to work when I hit middle school, eventually launching her own property management firm. Yes, the boss of her own firm. "I stayed in the workforce just in case something happened to my husband," she said, again ready for anything. Even then, she always had a hot meal ready for us when we came home. Always putting our needs first.

My parents have had a great marriage that's lasted almost forty years. My father always kissed my mother good-bye before he left for work, and always hugged and kissed her first thing when he came back home. Always.

Dad also called once or twice a day to check in at home, every time closing the conversation with "I love you." I only recall them fighting once, at the airport, over something really silly, and I remember my father buying roses and apologizing profusely afterward.

Through the years, no matter what challenges they faced, Mom and Dad always spoke positively of their marriage, and of the institution. They never pressured me to find a husband and have kids, though they wanted those things for me when I was ready. They wanted me to start a career, travel, experience life, and marry someone who was a loyal, loving match.

As well as my father provided for our family, Mom still put a lot of emphasis on being independent. "Don't rely on a man," she always said. "You can get married and fall in love and all, but don't rely on a man for your existence."

This was deeply ingrained in my psyche, so deeply that I stayed focused on schoolwork and only had one sort-of serious boyfriend in high school, and that guy was afraid to come over because my dad kept hunting rifles in a gun closet in our living room—locked up and unloaded, but present. That boyfriend, the nice, smart, athletic boy who'd had a crush on me since fourth grade, only saw me in class. The one time he came to my house was Christmas during our sophomore year of high school, when he dropped off a gift for me. He was so nervous he couldn't sit still the twenty minutes he was there, and then ran out of my house, forgetting to take home the gift I'd given him.

A few years later, I got into Northwestern University and studied journalism. I had your typical college hookups, but very few relationships. There were sorority date parties at the Texas Star Fajita Bar downtown or the Green Dolphin Street jazz club. But most of my college dates were focused on loftier goals, such as getting two PhDs before turning twenty-five, or running for office, or turning pro. One guy asked me out for dinner twice, and canceled both times at the last minute—after I already had my date-night outfit perfectly pressed—for meetings with NFL scouts.

I met one eager law student at a downtown nightclub. He called the next day. "Hey, are you into seafood?" he asked.

"Sure," I replied, thinking he was going to ask me on a date to an upscale restaurant recently written up in the *Chicago Tribune*, around the corner from where we met.

"You want to go to Red Lobster?" he cooed. We never went out.

After graduation, I set forth to cash in on that degree from Medill School of Journalism and forge a career as a writer. I was intent on making my parents proud, or at least feel that the thousands of dollars spent on tuition were worth it. So I went to the biggest playground for the best writers, New York City, with hopes of becoming the next Nora Ephron or Helen Gurley Brown. I was focused on my career, and figured that somewhere between working as an editor for a women's magazine and publishing my second and third novels, love and marriage would just happen.

I left for New York right after graduation, with my college roommate, Tina, and moved into a small cramped apartment in Midtown, like everyone else does when they get there. After interviewing at several fashion and entertainment magazines for assistant jobs, most of which involved very little writing or reporting and a lot of trips to the post office when not sitting in a windowless closet, I got a job at *Money* magazine, where my new boss allowed me from day one to write stories about business, stocks, mutual funds, and banks. The reporter position came with benefits and an annual salary big enough to cover rent, groceries, and a weekly manicure.

Our first apartment had no counter space, no cabinet space, and an oven that I was too scared to fire up for fear I'd set the entire building ablaze. Every meal we ate there was either microwaved or delivered in a white plastic bag with chopsticks.

After a year, I moved to a four-bedroom duplex on the Upper West Side that I split with three other girls. Our refrigerator was never really full, but we did have to divide shelf space among the four of us. Once I'd bought a few yogurts, a bag of grapes, and a soda, my allotted space was taken. Hard to buy groceries for a home-cooked meal if they don't fit in the refrigerator.

It's also hard to cook when three other people are trying to make oatmeal or pour wine in your cramped galley-style kitchen. Meals in that apartment were often ordered from Saigon Grill around the corner, or the pizza joint down the street.

After that apartment, Tina and I moved into a one-bedroom flat with a normal-size kitchen and bedroom, and a living room that was cut in half by a makeshift wall to make my cramped bedroom, just big enough for a queen-size bed. Tina, who occupied the main bedroom, and I agreed to cook one meal a week together, usually a Monday, but we stuck to things commonly found in a college dorm—pad thai, homemade pasta, tacos. But after a year, Tina moved back to Hawaii, and I settled into my own apartment on the Upper East Side.

My own place was a very functional first-floor studio in a low-rise building that used to be a bakery, perfect for an independent girl like me. It was big enough for a bed, a couch, a small table, and a desk, and large enough to entertain two other people comfortably, though entertaining was an afterthought, since most of my time was spent out on the town anyway. My apartment also had a full kitchen, a lovely patio, and . . . wait for it . . . a Walk. In. Closet. It was the most coveted of amenities, and a sign to all of my subway-commuting peers that after a decade of living in New York, I had officially "made it."

My first years in New York, I focused on my career, seeing the world, and collecting life experiences and stories to tell my grandchildren. I worked hard—late enough that I could expense dinner on the magazine's dime—and usually ended up having cocktails after work until it was time to go to sleep and start all over again the next day. The weekends were for meeting up with friends and going downtown to bars with velvet ropes and bouncers and overpriced drinks. Like every other single twentysomething girl in New York, I believed my life would be Carrie Bradshaw–esque, full of Cosmopolitans and brunches with girlfriends to talk about last night's conquest, until it all ends up in finding a Mr. Big to pay off my shoe debt. I had girlfriends and we had brunch, but there was no Mr. Big.

·   ·   ·

As I've gotten older, it seems to have gotten harder for women and men to connect romantically, and it's particularly hard in New York, where a person's worth is defined by their paycheck or iPhone contact list. The value of being a morally sound or spiritual person has declined, while the importance of being a top earner or socially connected, or owning a fantastic two-bedroom apartment south of Ninety-Sixth Street, has soared. Besides, New York is such a wonderful playground—Twenty-four-hour nightclubs! The Hamptons! Celebrity events! Models who work out at the same gym that I do!—that it makes the idea of moving to the suburbs to "grow up and settle down" less attractive. When people do find someone to date, they still have one eye looking out for a woman with bigger boobs or thinner thighs, or a guy with a bigger stock portfolio or apartment. People rarely love the one they're with in New York.

I dated bartenders, bankers, lawyers, and other well-to-do men during my early years there. One of the longest relationships I had was with a real estate entrepreneur, Steve, whom I met through friends. We had fun together, going to clubs and listening to music, but at thirty years old, he wasn't looking to settle down. It worked for a year because we made each other laugh and we enjoyed traveling together. But vacation isn't real life, and when the reality of the day-to-day with one person kicked in, he promptly cheated on me with a bisexual girl who would tolerate him sleeping with other women, primarily her roommate. I don't like to share—I don't even share mascara with other women, much less my boyfriend.

During the summer of 2006, I dated my next-door neighbor. I do not recommend that anyone date their neighbor. If you break up, you have to risk seeing that person every day when you're doing your laundry or walking the dog or ordering your nonfat latte at Starbucks. Or you have to move. And no ex-boyfriend is worth giving up good New York real estate.

I dated a Spanish chef, Armando. Armando was a decade older than I was, spent most of his life traveling and cooking through Europe, and owned a motorcycle. He cooked hundreds of Michelin-star-worthy meals for strangers, celebrities, and successful business-people, but he did not cook for me—not once in the year we dated. Not even popcorn. We ordered in for every dinner, and went out for breakfast. Though we ate well, the thing I remember most about that relationship is how much it centered around him. This was because every day, while serving beautiful food for beautiful people, he was treated like a rock star. Women think you're sexy because you cook and have a successful career. Men think you're smart because women think you're sexy (and you have a successful career). Oh, the power of a good plate of food.

Eventually, I became a reporter for the *New York Post* and the biggest, most influential gossip column in the world, Page Six. The column covers business, real estate, tech, nightlife, restaurants, celebrities, and relationships—divorces, breakups, marriages, hookups, threesomes, dates, flirting, and the conspicuous "canoodle." It's not unusual for me to go out four nights a week to parties, movie premieres, nightclubs, any place that celebrities would want to be.

I know, and write about, many of the most powerful people in New York: owners of restaurants, businesses, planes. I learned relatively quickly that people who own businesses are the foundation of wealth, as opposed to people who buy expensive things—those are just people with good credit. The pool of men surrounding me on a daily basis were mentioned in Page Six, or wanted to be mentioned in Page Six, or feared being mentioned in Page Six. I wasn't going to date the people I wrote about, or convince myself that Jay-Z was going to leave Beyoncé for me, or that Leonardo DiCaprio was going to pass over his latest Victoria's Secret Angel girlfriend in favor of me. And the wannabe models/actors/football stars/investment bankers/entrepreneurs/social climbers that wanted to be mentioned in Page Six weren't worthy of my time or column; they would eventually end up in Page Six, but for the wrong reasons—failed business, bad reality shows, embezzlement, or other tomfoolery.

I spent so much time surrounded by the type of guy I shouldn't date that I had no time to be around guys I should.

Don't get me wrong—I had a blast. I went to parties and met people and danced on tables and traveled to islands and drank champagne and watched fireworks being lit behind mansions and rode on yachts with international men of mystery. I covered elections and fashion shows and movie premieres and Super Bowls and celebrity weddings for my job. I had volumes of stories to tell my grandchildren that would read like they're from the archives of Bond films. But I had few opportunities to find a mate, to find love, settle down, and eventually start a family. I feared not being able to find the time, or the partner, to marry or have children with. Or even have the time to have and raise children on my own. I might keep writing and collecting stories, but when would I have grandchildren to tell the stories to?

This was an occupational hazard of working for New York's biggest entertainment column.

Which brings me to a cold Saturday in early March. I had suffered through a rough week: long hours at work and the death of my eighty-nine-year-old grandmother, whom I loved dearly. Plus, I "ran into" Chef Armando at a restaurant with his new girlfriend—taller, slimmer, and with bigger boobs. Of all the restaurants in New York City, I had to go to the one where someone who has seen me naked was eating truffled papardelle carbonara.

In full-throttle man-hating mode, I headed out for a boozy brunch with my friend Michelle. We drank a bloody Mary each, then another cocktail at another bar and another Bellini at our post-post-brunch bar afterward.

The Bellinis were followed by something mixed with gin at another restaurant, followed by a nap at Michelle's apartment in Chelsea. While I was deep in slumber, Michelle declared that I wouldn't be sleeping for long.

"We're going out."

"Why? I hate everybody," I spat, specifically referring to men, but figuring, why discriminate?

"There's no better excuse to go out than hating everyone," Michelle reasoned. "Let's meet new people to hate."

"I hate you," I snapped.

"Great, but hate me as you put on your shoes. Let's go."

We ventured around the block to the Half King, a Chelsea neighborhood pub. It was packed, and there were no tables available. "Great, maybe I can get that nap now."

"Not so fast," Michelle said. "Let's go around the corner. There's a place I know that's good."

Around the corner was Boutique Eat Shop, or BES, a restaurant next to an art gallery and across from a strip club. Inside, a man wearing dark black eyeliner, fishnet stockings, and a lace eye mask greeted us. "Welcome," he cooed. "Table for two, by the bar?"

Oversize images of the maître d' wearing his trademark fishnet stockings and women's lingerie hung along the walls in the restaurant. The speakers blared out old '90s club anthems. Another waiter wearing a Sgt. Pepper overcoat and leather pants took us to a high table at the bar by the window. He eventually brought us food and margaritas, then lingered with us over our drinks and shared girl talk as we ate.

As Michelle and I delved into our meal, in walked Eric (or E, as I like to call him). I was immediately struck by his surfer's build, sparkling blue eyes, and blond hair tucked behind his ear—he looked like Alexander Skarsgard from *True Blood* (without the fangs). He wore a leather-and-denim fitted jacket with long sleeves that hung past his wrists, which I liked. (It was very Prince. I love Prince.) Behind him was a tall blond woman with a spiky short haircut, leather jacket, and red lips. They looked like they were on a date. They also looked like they'd just come from a photo shoot. "Models," I said dismissively and turned back to the table.

E sidled up to the bar, ordered a Johnnie Walker Black, and sat contently while his lady friend hopped behind the turntables and DJed. I tried to concentrate on my margarita.

Michelle noticed me noticing him. "I'm going to the restroom," she said.

I warned Michelle not to do anything weird. "Do not tell him to talk to me on your way over there."

"I won't, I promise." And off she went.

Just when I think margarita and I are about to really get it on, E yells my way. "So you said your name is Stephanie, right?"

Apparently Michelle took some promises more seriously than others.

"Yep."

"Huh. I've dated a few Stephanies. They were all crazy."

I paused. He stared at me blankly, daring me to respond.

"Well," I say, turning my attention toward him, "sounds like you're picking the wrong Stephanies."

TWO

I had to cancel my first date with E because of a celebrity emergency. Due to my work at Page Six, my social life has often taken a backseat to that of the celebrities I write about. It takes a special man to understand that you're ditching him for Lindsay Lohan, and thankfully E was cool about the unique nature of my career.

When we finally did meet up for drinks a week later, he came equipped.

"You'll either think this is awesome, or never call me again," he told me after I'd finished off a requisite cocktail. "We're going to a James Bond–themed costume party. I brought wetsuits and a speargun."

An obvious homage to *Thunderball*.

The party was in honor of his best friend's fortieth birthday. Not only was he asking me to wear neck-to-ankle spandex; he wanted me to wear it in front of all his closest friends.

I thought about bailing, perhaps using work as an excuse *again*, but decided this was too good a story to miss out on telling my girlfriends.

"Well, I don't think this will do," I said in response to his invitation. "I think I need to rock a bikini under that wetsuit to give it the full Bond Girl effect. We need to go shopping."

After a quick stop to pick up an emergency swimsuit, we arrived in our secret agent finest. The crowd was, as expected, a mix of scantily clad women and well-suited men. Despite the awkwardness of meeting the majority of E's social circle on our first date—his friends grilling me on my career, family history, and why in the hell I agreed to go out to a James Bond–themed birthday party wearing a wetsuit on a first date with a "crazy stranger like E"—I never felt out of place. After the Bond party broke up, we ended up at a club (no longer adorned in surfwear). We danced, chatted, and laughed until the sun rose, and at 5:00 A.M. E put me into a cab like a gentleman, kissed me good morning, and sent me to my Upper East Side apartment.

Since he'd already seen me in a bikini, I didn't think E's second date offer for dinner at his place was too personal. I took a cab to East Sixth Street with a bottle of wine in hand and hoped that we wouldn't fall victim to the second-date slump—there was something there, and I hoped that it wasn't just a love of costumes.

His building was flanked by an Argentinian restaurant and a gay bar with a Russian theme, Eastern Bloc. E lived in the epicenter of the twentysomething nightlife, but as I rode the elevator up to his third-floor apartment, the sounds of sirens and drunken college students faded into the background. He greeted me with a smile, wearing a snug-fitting thermal Henley and dark-washed jeans.

"Come on in," he said, his piercing blue eyes crinkling at the corners. "Would you like a glass of wine?"

While he poured a glass of crisp white, I gingerly moved into his airy space, which smelled like vegetables sautéing in warm butter.

E's well-lit studio apartment was the bachelor pad of an adventure seeker. The brick walls were sparsely decorated, and a surfboard was parked in the corner near a platform queen-size bed, as if he was always ready to catch another wave, even if just in the Hudson River. "I'm a kitesurfer," he explained, walking me through the mechanics of the sport. "The surfboard is used for areas with big waves. I just got back from Maui"—which is known for consistent howling wind along its north shore. "I spent a month in Costa Rica learning a few years ago. I've since taken that board to Venezuela, Brazil, Morocco, and Vietnam."

My passport was up to date, I thought. Perhaps if things went well, there would be a vacation in our future. Maybe we'd get to reuse those wetsuits.

One large abstract painting in light blue and red hues hung on one wall, across from a comfy leather reading chair, where I imagined E sat to read the books I'd spied on his bookshelf: Dostoyevsky's *The Brothers Karamazov*, Salman Rushdie's *Midnight's Children*, and *Introduction to Japanese, vol. 1*.

A taxidermied deer head stared at me from its perch on the wall over the bed. "My grandfather's," he informed me, ". . . and my great-grandfather's," he said, pointing to the black bear rug that lay on the floor across from the bed. It was the home of a world traveler—little furniture or knickknacks, but a few prized artifacts of history, of culture, of places he'd either traveled to or wanted to.

E had an Oberheim keyboard stacked on the wall in its case, and a Taylor acoustic guitar set up near an oversized chair. I found out later he'd studied both as a kid, and was still proficient on both instruments. "I can still play 'Blackbird,' and anything strummed by Keith Richards, but I've gotten a bit rusty lately," he quipped.

My mind flashed forward to a few months into our relationship. I could see myself sitting in the oversize reading chair, my feet tucked under my legs, flipping through a *Travel + Leisure* magazine scouting our next kitesurfing adventure while he serenaded me with romantic lullabies on his Taylor. It would be the ideal East Village romance.

"You like scallops?" E asked, shaking me from my fantasy.

I did.

"I have fresh scallops here, but I'll need your help in shucking them."

Of course, I had no idea how that was done. But I liked that E didn't dictate dinner, he wanted me to share the cooking experience. Shucking scallops wasn't sexy or slow or neat, but it was fun and a little erotic. The slimy muscle sliding around in my hand, me cutting away the muscle with a small paring knife. Primitive, but romantic.

He plated the food with precision, as if he were presenting his scallops during dinner service at Nobu. He shaped the tomato compote with a ring mold, then carefully placed each scallop on top, moving slowly, like a surgeon. He wiped the sides of the plate clean with a napkin and then placed the large round dish in front of me. He waited for my verdict before he dove into the dinner. The sweet and tender scallops slid down my throat, chased by the tomato compote, tart and acidic. The meal was soft and sweet. It's what all second dates should taste like.

After a few glasses of wine, I found out that E was obsessed with *Star Wars,* James Bond, duck fat, kitesurfing, Johnnie Walker Black, and travel. He worked as a computer programmer, and created iPhone apps and websites and other things that make computing beautiful. He had no idea what Page Six was.

"I do not keep up with Kardashians," he said. That was such a turn-on.

So was E's cooking.

Our relationship transitioned easily from first dates to full-fledged romance. While I remained committed to eating anything E cooked, I wasn't quite as ready to reciprocate. It took four months before I got up the nerve to cook for him.

My first homemade meal for E was a Sunday-night dinner. I chose to make a goat cheese, fig, and caramelized onion tart, with a rich green salad, and for dessert, ice cream. I had never caramelized an onion, but according to the Internet, I only needed butter and an onion and a bit of sugar—I figured I couldn't mess it up that much. The tart included premade phyllo dough. There was no meat in the meal, which meant there was one less thing to worry about ruining.

My kitchen was not as lived-in as E's because I only used it to warm up coffee or arrange takeout. It was, however, perfect for a single gal on the go in the city, with pristine white cabinets and a fridge packed with water, a half-empty bottle of wine, a few cups of

Greek yogurt, ketchup and mustard bought when I moved in, and a carton of soy milk. My cupboards were stocked with dishes and cups to serve eight, but I repeatedly used the same favorite monogrammed mug for coffee and water. I had a toaster for toast and bagels, and a blender that only saw the light of day in the summer for smoothies and the occasional margarita. My countertop was pristine, and my dishwasher was empty. I had turned on the stove less than a dozen times since I'd moved in.

E arrived with wine in hand, kissing me on the cheek. I could have gone for a slightly more intense hello kiss but needed to keep my focus on those onions.

"You're fine," he said, intuiting my paranoia about improper cara-melizing technique. He opened a bottle of pinot noir and said some-thing about his subway ride to my place and his busy workweek. I didn't pay attention.

"Are you okay in there?" he asked. I reached for another glass of wine, uh-huh-ing my way through our one-sided conversation so that I could devote my entire attention to the now tannish onions in front of me.

I antisocially assembled the tarts and presented them to my now-official boyfriend. "I hope this is good," I said, preempting any ex-pectation that the food would be on par with E's concoctions.

It was . . . edible. Good, even. Sweet and savory.

"How is it?" I asked.

"I love it," he said.

"Really? What do you like about it?" I fished.

"The fact that you cooked it."

For the next eight months, I rested on the laurels of that tart. E con-tinued to do the cooking, I did the eating. We took a trip to Miami that he'd promised me during our first meeting at BES, and that trip was followed by a ten-day wine-tasting and kitesurfing jaunt to South Africa and a two-week trip to Brazil. We attended movie premieres together, a perk of my job, and celebrated birthdays together with dinners out at our favorite restaurants. I followed him to the beach on windy days to watch him kitesurf up and down the coast, and he bought me kitesurfing lessons so I would hopefully enjoy the sport as much as he did.

And then we moved in together, a year after dating, and everything changed. Things got real once we were forced to share a kitchen.

THREE

To watch my mother make a sandwich for my father was a study in holy matrimony.

The scene played out the same, year after year, sandwich after sandwich. My father would come into the kitchen and, without saying a word, my mother would know exactly what it was he had come in search of.

"You want a turkey sandwich?" Mom asked him.

Dad would nod and then turn and walk toward the family room, careful not to be in her way as she worked her magic.

What proceeded was an intricate but well-rehearsed dance: My mother pulled tomatoes, lettuce, and Miracle Whip from the refrigerator. Then she reached into the cupboard for a loaf of white bread. Mom moved gingerly around the counter, unhurried, calmly lining up her ingredients, her props for her well-honed choreography. She grabbed a butter knife from the drawer. Then, she dove in.

Mom spread a thin layer of Miracle Whip on the soft white bread. She knew not to toast the bread because Dad wanted his bread a bit chewy. She tore leaves of iceberg lettuce from the head, knowing exactly how many layers of lettuce to stack on the bread without it getting too thick. She sliced up a tomato in her hand, red juice running down her soft fingers as she ran the knife through a juicy piece of fruit fresh from the garden, and layered it on the lettuce. She pulled out slices of turkey breast and stacked the meat on top. Finally, she cut his sandwich on the diagonal and placed either a handful of potato chips or a scoop of potato salad on the side.

Dad knew this dance too; after five minutes passed he'd reappear in the kitchen to take his sandwich back to the family room.

Twenty minutes later, he'd return with an empty plate.

My parents have been married for thirty-eight years. There must have been thousands of turkey sandwiches just like this one in their years of wedded bliss. I have to think that my dad stuck around, in some small part, because his wife knew exactly how he liked his turkey sandwiches.

And this is why I wanted to take on this challenge for E.

If I was going to be an equal partner in this relationship, and eventually in our family, I needed to learn how food was prepared. I needed to know how to make nutritious meals to feed myself and my family. Cooking is power. Food is nutrition. It's medicine. It can reunite families and be a peace offering between strangers.

When a woman cooks for her family, she has the power to take care of herself, nurture her body, feed her family. She can make herself more fertile, ward against cancer, provide energy for a workout, or simply satisfy a sweet tooth. She can help her husband lower his cholesterol or prep for a big day at the office. She has the power to satisfy his hunger, his lust, his cravings. And how do you expect your children to survive if you don't know how to make chicken noodle soup that's not out of a can? They can't live on peanut butter and jelly alone.

I needed to know how to make cakes to celebrate birthdays and stellar report cards, know how to bake cookies for my kid's bake sale so she felt like Mommy cared about her and her school, and know what to make when my kids needed to do well on exams.

I needed to know these things to become a well-rounded, giving human being.

I could start to accomplish this by learning to make delicious sandwiches, one sandwich at a time.

·   ·   ·

For E and me, sandwiches became our "thing." Whether we were watching a movie or cuddling in bed, E would request a sandwich. Marvin Gaye wooed women with "Let's get it on"—E seduced me with "How about a sandwich?"

I had never truly learned the magic of spices, the wonder of condiments, the proper way to roast a chicken—but I could make a sandwich. That is exactly what I did one lazy Sunday afternoon as E broke in our new couch.

A simple sandwich was more than a sandwich, it was a thank-you for all the beautiful meals he'd whipped up: the duck confit, the beautifully seared scallops, the roast leg of lamb, the whole roasted fish he'd presented artfully at dinnertime. This sandwich was a promise that our new life together would be equal, that I'd put in the same amount of effort to take care of him as he did me, and it was a token of my love for him. I barraged him with questions: "Mustard? Mayo? Both?" I asked how he liked his sandwich cut—my father had always been particularly fond of the diagonal cut, for example. (These were things I should know about the man I was living with, like how he takes his coffee.) And, of course, I stressed over the proper meat-to-cheese ratio, and the perfect sizing of each crunchy lettuce leaf.

With shaky hands I presented my masterpiece: turkey and Swiss on white bread with a smear of Dijon.

E devoured it as if it were his last supper, posting photos of his lunch on Facebook. And then he turned to me and said:

"Honey, you are three hundred sandwiches away from an engagement ring."

I stood in the kitchen, mouth agape. Did he *really* just say that? Was that a proposal to propose? Did he really want me to make him 300 sandwiches to *earn* an engagement ring?

There was a knee-jerk reaction to throw a sandwich in his general direction, and an internal monologue on my part that quoted the too-too-wise-for-his-age Arnold Jackson, *"What'chu talkin' 'bout, Willis?"*

But after a deep breath and a flash of E's enormous smile, I thought about his words. E appreciated that I'd done something nice for him. Aren't happy marriages made up of a lifetime of doing the things that make your partner happy?

It would not be the worst idea to make 300 sandwiches for E. Not because I wanted him to propose (although I did), but because I loved him, and I loved that feeling of taking care of him. Each of the 300 sandwiches would be my way of saying "I love you."

Aside from getting engaged, I wondered what could happen in our relationship over the course of 300 sandwiches. How many breakfast sandwiches would we eat together in bed, or while sipping coffee and drooling over overpriced real estate listings? How many s'mores would we devour in front of the fireplace on snowboarding trips? How many debates would rage over our different preferences for meat or bread? How many fights would end with makeup sandwiches? How many anniversaries, birthdays, holidays, promotions, and (God forbid) funerals would we celebrate—over sandwiches?

Our relationship, and my skills in the kitchen, would grow in that time. This could only make me a better cook and us a more closely bonded couple. Right?

"Okay," I said. "I'll make you two hundred ninety-nine more."

sandwich

#1

THE BEGINNING—TURKEY AND SWISS ON COUNTRY WHITE

The turkey and Swiss was the very first sandwich I made for E. I was nervous that it wasn't good enough. Apparently it was. With #1 down, I just had 299 more to go.

**2 slices bread
1 tablespoon Dijon mustard
4 or 5 slices Swiss cheese
4 or 5 slices turkey
2 or 3 Bibb lettuce leaves
1 pickle**

Word of advice: Follow along, but adjust your assembly and ingredients to your liking, keeping in mind I'm no pro. My sandwiches were made to be loved, not perfected.

Toast bread. Smooth mustard on one piece. Layer on Swiss cheese, then meat, then lettuce. Top with other piece of bread. Cut on the diagonal. Add pickle on the side. Makes 1 sandwich.

Sure, this sandwich is as basic as it gets, but this culinary dunce had to start somewhere. As I went along, I got better in the kitchen. I experimented more with flavors and ingredients. The sandwiches became more adventurous. And delicious. To that end, I've arranged the recipes in this book thematically rather than chronologically— that way you won't have to wait too long for a real "meaty" one.

FOUR

The idea for documenting all 300 sandwiches into a blog came as most great ideas do—over margaritas, sketched out on a napkin. After we told the idea to E's best friend, Graham, his first reaction to the ridiculousness of anyone making anyone else 300 sandwiches for anything was: "That's a great idea for a blog."

I bought the 300sandwiches.com URL immediately.

I would record every sandwich I made for my boyfriend and track our relationship—our adventures, our days in, our nights out, our vacations, and my journey as I learned to be a better chef, and the laughs, the adventures, and the feminist controversy that surrounded my quest. If this little project ended in an engagement ring, all the better. If not, at least we'd have a digital cookbook to look back on and share with our family and friends and the entire Internet-accessible world.

I didn't know how to cook a steak or season fish. I didn't own a decent camera. But I had a credit card, access to tons of food blogs and magazines, and a mission. And so I got cooking. And blogging.

But before I started documenting our meals for all the world to see, I wanted to establish some house rules of sandwich making with the man who would be eating them.

We decided early in negotiations that breakfast, lunch, dinner, and dessert sandwiches were all game.

E had to have at least one bite of any sandwich made. And, he added, "You can't just make three hundred sandwiches at once for a bunch of my friends. They have to be three hundred sandwiches for me."

Fair enough. After all, he would be the one buying the ring.

This also gave me some leeway on my less successful endeavors. Even if a sandwich failed, as long as I made it for E, it still counted.

To further complicate matters, each sandwich had to be distinctly different. I could do multiple *types* of, say, peanut butter and jelly, but I had to vary at least two ingredients and the type of bread. And, when applicable, the preparation.

Most important, we defined the term *sandwich* for our challenge purposes: two pieces of bread or breadlike items, with filling, usually portable.

"Or a wrap with filling," I said, since a wrap was a portable hand-held meal like a sandwich.

"Okay," E said.

"Do burgers qualify?" I asked.

"Absolutely. Sloppy Joes, meatball sliders," he said. "They all count."

"What about burritos?"

"Good question," E said. "Let's Google it."

As it turns out, burritos are a complicated issue. In 2006, a Massachusetts court ruled that a burrito is not a sandwich in a dispute between Panera Bread and Qdoba Mexican Grill. The judge in the case argued that a sandwich is not understood to include tacos, quesadillas, or burritos, which are typically made with a single tortilla and stuffed with a choice filling of meat, rice, and beans.

"But burritos are like wraps," I said.

"I'll give you this one," he said, giving me more options to choose from to make 300 different sandwiches. "They count."

Quesadillas? "Hmmm, it can be two pieces of bread with filling. But for the sake of this experiment I vote no."

Tacos? "Definitely not."

E and I spent a week debating whether or not crepes qualified. We emailed several French friends asking them what they thought. "Oui," they said. Crepes were fair game.

Italian sausage subs and hot dogs? Sandwiches.

I would attempt to make as many of the ingredients as possible from scratch, including the majority of sauces, marinades, and cookies. Of the goods that were store-bought—bread, fish, cheese—we chose the freshest option. I avoided frozen or canned foods when possible, and looked for locally grown or farm-fresh goods when time and assembly permitted.

E also considered certain foods absolutely unacceptable on a sandwich. I don't mean he didn't prefer them. I mean hated. Loathed. Detested.

"There are things I simply will not eat on a sandwich," he said.

I would come to know intimately (and resent) this list of foods prohibited from being used on a sandwich:

THE FORBIDDEN FOODS LIST

Sliced avocado	Raw tomatoes
Broccoli	Peas
Spinach	Kale
Mushrooms	Blueberries
Anything with the word *sprouts* in it	Raisins
(bean, alfalfa, Brussels, etc.)	Olives
Cauliflower	Frisée

"I can't use greens on sandwiches?" I asked.

"Of course you can, just romaine or arugula. Or cabbage. Or mixed greens. But no kale or spinach. Ick."

"How can someone who cooks so beautifully discriminate against leafy greens? And why don't you like broccoli?" I asked.

"It's just gross. The texture is awful. It is the worst green in existence. Even the smell of it is gross."

I understood that everyone has their preferences. When you go to a restaurant or a deli or a coffee shop, and someone produces food or a beverage to your liking, you're satisfied.

When my bagel is toasted dark enough and there's the perfect spread of jelly on top, or when my mom makes a cobbler just the way I like it—heavy on the fruit and lighter on the dough—it makes me feel happy. As if I'm queen of my own universe.

For E, not using raw tomatoes and avoiding greens made him happy.

And I, as his partner, his hoping-to-be wife, should make his next 299 sandwiches as he preferred.

"All right, no broccoli. Or kale. Or spinach," I said.

Time to get to work.

FORBIDDEN SANDWICHES

I hadn't eaten a stalk of broccoli since E and I started dating. Well, that's not true. I could eat it on the sly when out with friends, or occasionally when E and I ate out, but only under the condition that our plates were completely separate.

I wanted to marry E, but that didn't mean I wanted to divorce my favorite vegetables in the process.

Whenever E was out of town or wasn't available for dinner, I would make what I call the Forbidden Sandwich—from goods on his Forbidden Foods list that I loved.

Spinach was one of my favorite vegetables.

"NEVER ON ANYTHING. EVER," E declared. "It's gross, and so was Popeye."

"Wasn't he a hero?" I asked.

"He had nonexistent biceps, huge forearms, and an obvious speech impediment. . . . Weird."

Brussels sprouts sautéed in sage butter were a perfect complement to a pumpkin soup we made for a fall dinner.

When I suggested using Brussels sprouts for a grilled cheese sandwich, E turned up his lip in disgust.

I waved one of the cooked, buttery sprouts under his nose, hoping he'd take just a bite, "just a little itty bite. . . ."

"I swear I will grab a sprout out of the hot pan with my bare hands and throw that at you if you don't get it out of here," E said.

I made the damn sandwich anyway. I was that hungry. Soup does not a full stomach make.

Zucchini also wasn't allowed in our house. But when I went home to see my parents in Michigan, I wolfed down a fried zucchini, ricotta, and tomato sandwich on pretzel bread that my mother and I put together. Delish.

And then I got real ballsy—while E was away on a kitesurfing vacation, I made the ultimate forbidden sandwich: alfalfa sprouts with raw avocado AND raw tomatoes. It was an explosion of Forbidden Foods on toast. And, boy, was it good. People might have thought E and I were on the verge of breaking up, considering how many Forbidden Foods were on that piece of toast. But no. I was just hungry. And missing my favorite vegetables.

Forbidden *sandwich*

#1

BROCCOLI GRILLED CHEESE

E hates broccoli. "It smells like rot," he says. "You get a good meal at a Chinese restaurant, and the carrots and celery and peppers are delicious. And then they throw broccoli in there. Ick." This logic makes no sense to me. I love broccoli—sautéed with butter, or with grilled cheese. When E was out of town, I devoured one of these broccoli grilled cheese sandwiches while home alone.

1 cup chopped broccoli
2 tablespoons olive oil
1 garlic clove, smashed
1 tablespoon mayonnaise
½ cup shredded cheese
of your choice (I like Monterey Jack)
1 tablespoon unsalted butter
2 slices bread
salt and pepper
Tabasco (optional)

Sauté the chopped broccoli in a medium saucepan with the olive oil and garlic, stirring frequently, until the broccoli is tender, 3 to 5 minutes. Remove from heat and place in a bowl with the mayonnaise and shredded cheese. Stir together. Spread butter on one side of both slices of bread. With the butter side facing the plate, spread the broccoli-cheese mixture on one slice. Season with salt and pepper (and Tabasco, if desired). Top with the other slice, butter side up, and toast in a pan on medium heat until golden brown. Makes 1 sandwich. Yep, just one. For me. Ha! (You want two? Just double the recipe.)

SPINACH, MUSHROOM, AND EGG-WHITE WRAP

Spinach and mushrooms together will never be eaten by E. But when he's away, I eat them together, because they're delicious. And I will feel "strong to the finish, 'cause I eats me spinach." Just like Popeye. Without the weird arms, though.

2 tablespoons olive oil
½ garlic clove, chopped
½ cup chopped mushrooms
½ teaspoon chopped fresh parsley (optional)
½ teaspoon chopped fresh oregano (optional)
salt and pepper
4 egg whites
handful of baby spinach leaves (about ½ cup)
1 large tortilla
1 teaspoon unsalted butter

Heat the oil and garlic in a medium pan on medium-high heat. Toss in the mushrooms and sauté about 2 minutes, stirring frequently. Add the chopped parsley and oregano (if desired), and season with salt and pepper. Push the mushrooms to one side of the pan and pour the egg whites on the other side. Sprinkle the spinach leaves on top. Cook until the eggs are the desired firmness and the spinach until leaves wilt (about 2 minutes). Stir the eggs and vegetables to combine at the end of cooking, and remove from heat.

Toast the tortilla until soft and warm. Lay it flat and spread the egg and vegetable mixture down the middle. Wrap the left and right sides inward, then tuck in the top and bottom. To help hold the wrap together, lightly butter the ends where they will meet. Cut in half and enjoy. Makes 1 wrap.

FRIED ZUCCHINI AND SLICED TOMATO ON PRETZEL ROLL

This is one of my mother's favorite summertime dishes—fresh zucchini, fried up crisp, and juicy tomatoes from the garden, all piled on a pretzel bun with ricotta. It's a great snack while reading magazines on the front porch in July.

vegetable oil for frying
1 cup flour
¾ teaspoon celery salt
1 teaspoon garlic salt
1 teaspoon paprika
1 egg
1 egg white
2 medium zucchinis, sliced
1 to 2 tablespoons unsalted butter
4 pretzel buns
¼ cup ricotta cheese
1 medium tomato, sliced
hot sauce (optional)

In a medium frying pan, pour an inch of vegetable oil and heat over medium heat. In a small shallow bowl, mix the flour, celery salt, garlic salt, and paprika. In another bowl, beat the egg with the egg white until well combined. Dip the zucchini slices into the egg wash, then into the flour mixture, then fry in the hot oil. (The oil is hot enough if it sizzles and bubbles when the first slice of zucchini hits it.) Cook about 4 minutes each side until brown, flipping once. Remove from the oil with a slotted spoon and drain on a paper-towel-lined plate.

Melt a tablespoon or two of butter in a large pan and toast the buns on medium heat. Spread a thin layer of ricotta cheese on both sides of the buns. On the bottom halves, layer zucchini and tomato slices. Sprinkle with hot sauce. Place the top buns on top of the sandwiches. Makes 4 sandwiches.

BRUSSELS SPROUTS GRILLED CHEESE

Chopped Brussels sprouts, cheese, and butter nestled in crusty warm bread? What could be better? Maybe Mediterranean sunsets viewed from a ninety-foot yacht. I guess. But, hey, this will do.

2 cups Brussels sprouts
2 to 3 tablespoons unsalted butter
½ medium onion, sliced
2 tablespoons chopped fresh sage
generous pinch kosher salt
1 teaspoon black pepper
generous pinch red pepper flakes (optional)
4 slices crusty wheat bread
4 to 6 slices fontina cheese

Prepare the Brussels sprouts: Boil the sprouts in water for 6 to 8 minutes. Drain in a colander and set aside. In a nonstick pan over low to medium heat, melt the butter, then add the onion and cook until slightly browned, about 3 minutes. Add the sage. After about 5 minutes, add the Brussels sprouts. Stir in the kosher salt and pepper (and red pepper flakes if you're feeling spicy). Sauté another 6 to 8 minutes, until almost charred. Remove from heat. Save the pan and its butter.

Shred the Brussels sprouts. On the bottom slices of bread, lay cheese and a generous scoop of shredded sprouts. Sprinkle with more black pepper, top with more cheese, and finish each with another slice of bread.

Brown the sandwiches in the pan—yes, the one coated in the sage butter, trust me—until the cheese is melted and the bread is browned, about 3 minutes on each side. Remove from heat and slice in half. Makes 2 sandwiches.

ALFALFA SPROUTS, TOMATO, AND AVOCADO ON WHOLE WHEAT

A medley of E's Forbidden Foods—sprouts, tomato, sliced avocado—between two pieces of bread. It's the simplest healthy veggie sandwich possible. E doesn't know what he's missing.

2 slices whole wheat bread
1 medium tomato, chopped
½ avocado, cubed
¼ cup chopped cucumber
black pepper
1 tablespoon chopped fresh cilantro
1 tablespoon olive oil
2 tablespoons whipped cream cheese
handful alfalfa sprouts (about ⅓ cup)

Toast the bread. Place the tomato, avocado, cucumber, black pepper, cilantro, and olive oil in a small bowl. Combine with a fork. Spread cream cheese on both slices of bread. Put the alfalfa sprouts on the bottom piece of bread and top with a scoop of the avocado/tomato mixture. Finish with the other slice of bread. Makes 1 sandwich.

FIVE

"But can you cook?" my mother asked when I called to tell her about our proposal-to-propose arrangement.

"Not as well as E can," I responded, pacing around my kitchen as we spoke. Maybe this wasn't such a good idea.

"So, three hundred different sandwiches. Can you even think of three hundred sandwiches?"

"There are a lot of sandwiches I could make; I can make different breakfast sandwiches, dinner sandwiches, open-faced sandwiches."

"Those count?"

"Yup."

"Huh," Mom said.

My parents knew E and I were serious. We were living together, after all, and so far very happily. My mother liked what she knew of E because he treated me well, and he always did what he said he was going to do. "He reminds me of your father," she said.

Mom told Dad about the blog. "Your daughter says she's going to make three hundred sandwiches in order to get an engagement ring from E," she said, explaining the circumstances under which my boyfriend of a year, who had barely met my parents, had said he would propose to me.

My father's reaction was laughter. His reaction to most things was laughter.

And then, he thought hard about how many sandwiches I could come up with. "That's a lot of sandwiches. Quite the challenge," he said. (This coming from the man who proposed on the first date.)

"How long do you think it will take you to make three hundred sandwiches?" Mom asked.

"Not sure. I'm guessing a little over a year, if I do four or five a week."

"And will you be ready to be married in a year?" she asked. "Or, can you wait another year for him to be ready to be married?"

I hadn't thought that far ahead. I was too busy thinking up sandwich ideas and trying to get my site live before I started cooking. I assumed we would be.

"I would hope, after three hundred sandwiches, he'd be ready to propose. A deal is a deal. And why *wouldn't* he marry me? What other woman would make him that many sandwiches?"

"None that I can think of," Mom said. "But why can't he make you a sandwich?"

"Because he's too busy making me duck, lamb, and lobster every night."

"Ah." Mom let out a chuckle.

I stood by the sink in our kitchen. Dirty dishes from last night's dinner—duck breast with roasted tomatoes—were still soaking.

"Well," Mom said. "Let's see how many sandwiches we can come up with to get you started."

I got a text from my father a few days after my conversation with Mom.

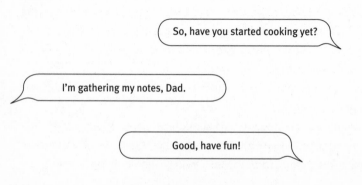

So, have you started cooking yet?

I'm gathering my notes, Dad.

Good, have fun!

While I got busy stocking our refrigerator with meat, vegetables, and condiments, E got busy designing my website. I invested in a camera good enough for high-quality food photography, the same model I'd borrowed from a friend for a vacation and was comfortable enough with to use for the blog. Then, I got to work.

If I were to "earn" this ring through sandwiches and entertain a reading public with a blog, I wanted my sandwiches to look good enough to eat right off the computer monitor.

Of my first ten sandwiches, maybe half were worthy of a second grader's lunch box.

Sandwich #1, the classic turkey and Swiss, was hard to get wrong. But I still fretted over it as much as that very first goat cheese tart I cooked for E. I was unsure if I was using the right type of Swiss cheese, or the right bread, or if he was going to eat Bibb lettuce, since E was picky about his greens. You can't really discriminate against Bibb lettuce, could you?

Yet, he ate the finished product. And he wanted 299 more.

The second sandwich was an easy ice cream sandwich with premade ginger wafers and a dollop of ice cream. No sweat.

Sandwich #3 was a veggie delight with pepper. Nothing special. Edible. As per our rules, the sandwiches didn't all have to be gourmet to count toward the 300 . . . E just had to have a bite.

I got cocky with sandwich #4—I tried to challenge myself and ended up in tears.

Sandwich #4, cooked on a hot July night after work, was a swordfish sandwich with roasted yellow peppers and a jalapeño emulsion that E had made many times from the Eric Ripert cookbook *On the Line*. We thought a solid fish sandwich coupled with that delicious flavoring would make a great combo. Swordfish is one of my favorites when ordering at a seafood restaurant. I had no idea how to cook it, but I knew enough to ask E for help. E volunteered to make the emulsion, and I prepared the fish.

We both set up camp in the kitchen, pulling herbs and the fish from the refrigerator and scattering our countertop with small bottles of seasoning from our cabinets. The swordfish came in one large steak that weighed close to a pound. It would barely fit in the largest skillet we owned, but I figured I'd just smash in the sides. I cranked up the heat on the stove.

"Honey, did you season the fish first?"

"Nope, but let me get on that." I turned off the heat, a little embarrassed I'd forgotten this crucial step in front of E.

"I was thinking salt and pepper and maybe some parsley."

E had other opinions. "Maybe cumin?" he asked. "What about cilantro?"

I sprinkled a dash of cayenne pepper and some cumin all over the fish, and finished it with salt and pepper.

I then moved the entire swordfish steak into the skillet.

"Wait, stop. Take it out of the pan. Aren't you going to cut the fish into sandwich-size fillets so it fits perfectly on the bread? It's easier to cut it now while it's raw."

"Okayy . . . fine." Could I do anything right?

I placed the fish back on the cutting board, grabbed a small paring knife, and started to make my way around the fish. The thirteen-ounce swordfish fillet was now divided into two small fillets about six ounces each, cut into uneven discs slightly larger than the slices of crusty Italian bread I planned to use for the sandwiches.

"While that cooks, I'll handle the emulsion," E volunteered. Finally, some help I could use.

I nervously plopped the fish onto the hot skillet, the sound of searing meat grating against my ears like nails on a chalkboard. "Am I good?" I asked E.

"You're fine."

As the swordfish cooked, I placed bread for the bottom slices of our sandwiches on plates.

Just as I was about to pull the fish out of the skillet, E turned in horror: "Did you toast the bread first?"

I grew frustrated. "Do you want to do this yourself?"

"No, you're doing great! It looks perfect," he encouraged.

When the swordfish was ready, I fumbled with tongs to dig it from the skillet. The fish was slippery and I worried I might get burned by a splatter of oil from the pan. "Just get after it," E encouraged. "Be quick!"

After several false starts, I placed the swordfish steaks on the cutting board, then popped two slices of crusty bread in the toaster.

I placed the toasted bread on a plate, and E spooned some of the jalapeño emulsion over it. I grabbed a fistful of arugula to place on the bread.

"Wait, aren't you gonna do anything with the greens before you add them? Maybe a little vinaigrette? Olive oil? Lemon juice, maybe?" E asked.

"Seriously?!"

"Honey, plain arugula on toast? How about this: two parts olive oil and one part vinegar, maybe a little bit of mustard, shallot, and some citrus, season to taste with salt and pepper. Take it to the next level. It'll take one minute tops."

Did I have to think this much about crafting a simple sandwich? And wouldn't the emulsion wet the greens enough to make them more palatable?

I angrily stirred olive oil, along with the rest of the ingredients E had rattled off, into a suitable dressing, then spooned it over the greens in a larger bowl. I placed forkfuls of arugula on the bread, layered on the swordfish, the peppers, and some more emulsion. E took a look at the plate before he served dinner, wiping up any stray emulsion or olive oil that had dirtied it before digging in.

"There. Now isn't that delicious?"

It was. But it was also so . . . complex. And anxiety-inducing, given that I had done so many things wrong in E's eyes. Was every sandwich going to be like this?

Sandwich #10, my first crack at sloppy Joes, was a disappointment. They were not-so-sloppy Joes, crumbly and dry like thick meaty beads of overdone couscous.

I borrowed Rachael Ray's famed "Messy Giuseppe" recipe, because I wanted a sloppy Joe that was wet, dripping saucy tomato juice all over the bun. Rachael had made it all look so easy. I used turkey meat instead of ground beef or ground sausage, in an effort to keep it healthy. But somehow I combined the wrong ratio of meat to sauce, adding only half of the amount of tomatoes I needed, and ended up with a crumbly meat mess.

When I spooned the meat onto the roll, the dry mixture tumbled right out of the sides instead of sticking together in its own tomato sauce, since there was really no sauce. "Those are some sad-looking sloppy Joes," E said. The photo I took of the sandwich for the blog was even sadder—at night, in the dark, on a scratched white plate, with the bun completely lopsided. The sloppy Joe looked like a dead Pac-Man with his guts spilling on the floor.

After that, I was too nervous to try to cook meat for a while. I made a fried green tomato with mozzarella sandwich on toasted wheat bread, another riff on a summertime staple my mom would make for me during my childhood summers in Michigan. I called her while I made them to make sure I'd used enough batter and oil. I experimented with breakfast sandwiches—the best was open-faced with ricotta, fresh fruit, mint, and honey. It was at this point that I learned E does not like blueberries. Who doesn't like blueberries? Particularly, who from Michigan, such as E, where blueberry farms are everywhere, doesn't like blueberries?

Sandwich #19 gave me hope that I might be able to do something right. E and I had worked late that night and were in the mood for something hearty. I also wanted to make something that really showed my appreciation for his being relatively patient with me as I embarked on this 300 project. And I wanted something that paired well with red wine. I suggested my first steak sandwich: prime rib with caramelized onions on a rosemary roll.

I caramelized some onions—by now I at least felt comfortable enough to caramelize onions and look away from the stove for a few minutes at a time.

"Do you want to do the meat or should I?" I asked.

"I think you've got it," E said, with more compassion than he'd showed while instructing me how to cook swordfish.

According to E, the key with steak is using medium-high heat to sear it for a few minutes on each side, basting continuously with butter, olive oil, and some aromatics like rosemary or maybe thyme. Most important, after cooking it needs to rest for 10 minutes under aluminum foil. "I learned that from sitting at the counter at Momofuku Noodle Bar," E said, speaking of one of our favorite restaurants, run by super-talented, so-cool-you-want-to-invite-him-to-your-backyard-barbecue-every-weekend chef David Chang. "Seriously, it's how they all do it." They all, meaning all the James Beard Award–winning, media-darling, bourbon-drinking, pork belly–serving chefs.

But we had a very thick steak, so I had to let it cook for a bit longer. I feared overcooking it the entire time.

"No, no, you're doing just fine," E said.

But I wasn't. I felt more insecure with E in the kitchen than when left alone to screw up in solitude. With every correction, I doubted my abilities as a chef. As a girlfriend. As a future wife and mother. I imagined all the failed Fourth of July barbecues in years to come. The barely edible summer dinners for friends who would politely move the food around their plate until it looked somewhat eaten. The school lunches my kids would gladly exchange for pudding packs.

"Here," E said, grabbing a spoon from the cupboard. "Take the spoon, tip the pan toward you, and ladle the butter and juice that pools at the bottom over the steak, like this," he demonstrated. "That way you baste the meat in that flavorful butter and fat so it stays juicy."

The steak was just as moist as he promised.

This was a manly sandwich—an undainty, meaty, hearty, savory steak sandwich dripping with spicy flavor. E loved the combination of sweet caramelized onions and steak with seedy spicy mustard.

"This is your best sandwich yet," he said. Maybe I could cook. Maybe my future offspring wouldn't be so quick to trade their lunches after all.

Those first 20 sandwiches were rich. The oily emulsions, buttery steaks, fried accents, and added meat and cheese in my diet left me feeling bloated. If I kept going at this rate, by the time my 300th sandwich came to fruition, I'd need a new wardrobe to go with my engagement ring.

Sandwich #24, my biggest mistake, was a healthy, no-fat, no-flavor recipe from a fitness magazine—shrimp and couscous pita sandwiches with mango, tomato, and avocado. The recipe was included in a roundup called "400-Calorie or Less Dinners." Any dish that markets itself as having as few calories as possible is probably going to have as little taste as possible. See celery, low-fat potato chips, iceberg lettuce, and fat-free frozen yogurt.

The recipe called for spinach, but I had to omit the leafy green because it's on E's list of forbidden veggies. Technically, avocado and tomato were on the forbidden list too, but this sandwich needed as many vegetables as possible to add flavor, plus the avocado provided some healthy fats. I assumed E would pick the vegetables out if they were offensive to his palate. I also forgot to include the jalapeño the recipe called for, because . . . I just forgot.

I didn't follow the directions exactly, but I doubt that would have made a difference. There was something about foil pockets mentioned, but I figured that as long as I made the couscous per the instructions on the box, cooked the shrimp, and then mixed both with the cold veggies and stuffed the entire mixture into pita pockets, I could call it dinner. Instead, the sandwich tasted like I'd thrown together whatever was available in our fridge—fresh and not so fresh.

I asked E how it was.

"Well, it's food," he replied.

The pita tasted like cardboard, the raggedy arugula tasted like weeds. The mango and tomato weren't juicy, and the avocado and couscous just made the whole thing mushy and mealy. And the shrimp, well, I might as well have gone fishing in the East River and pulled out whatever mercury-laden mutated fish I found to cook instead. It would have had more flavor.

That night, E and I went out for dinner.

Sandwich #27 marked a turning point in my journey—someone besides E was subject to my culinary experimentation. Tina, my college and post-college roommate until she left me for Hawaii, had come to visit.

"I can't believe you're making him three hundred sandwiches. That's a lot of sandwiches. Can you eat all of them?"

"Probably not," I warned. "But I can make them."

"Can't you just order three hundred sandwiches and give them to him, and tell him you made them?"

A few months ago I would have probably gone that route, but now I had something to prove. To myself, and apparently to my ex-roommate. I started with breakfast.

I made poached eggs and bacon sandwiches on English muffins for the three of us. E had taught me to poach eggs without those half-moon molds—near-boiling-but-not-rolling water with a little bit of vinegar, then swirling the water around with a spoon, plopping a cracked egg in the middle; letting the water shape the white of the egg around itself, cooking it as it twirled; and removing it when it had formed into a mass that resembled a mozzarella ball.

I placed the poached egg carefully on an English muffin topped with greens, bacon, and fresh chives. This, with a warm mug of coffee and a bowl of fresh fruit, was a breakfast that rivaled the best mid-priced hotel in town.

"You never cooked for me like this when we were roommates," Tina said. Point. Proven.

Once someone I was not sleeping with had eaten my cooking and survived, I threw our first dinner party. Before I started cooking, E and I had specific roles when we hosted dinner parties. E was the executive chef/master of all things oven, refrigerator, and range top. I was, at best, a line cook in *his* kitchen. Actually, I was of better use managing the front-of-house duties. I handled cleanup, dish and glass management, table settings, and house coat check.

I decided to step out of my shell just once. For a Saturday-evening party, complete with guests, wine, food—and me, with shaking hands and a burgeoning anxiety attack when it came to the prospect of feeding other people. I decided paninis would be a safe bet. Melted cheese is always a crowd-pleaser—hell, even when cheese is burnt it's good.

The close friends who knew about the blog had promised to keep an open mind about my cooking, and arrived at our apartment, peckish from their cross-river commute. E filled wine glasses while I prepped sandwiches in the kitchen, stacking cheese and vegetables onto nutty whole-grain breads.

I served #34, a bacon, Manchego, and arugula panini, and #35, a panini stuffed with basil, mozzarella, and caramelized onion (notice I stick with what I do well). They went quickly. The basil brightened up the sweet caramelized onion with the mozzarella. The bacon, arugula, and Manchego panini was so good, even E's vegetarian cousin had a bite.

"I would marry you after this one sandwich! Forget the two hundred and ninety-nine others!" one of E's friends declared.

If I could satisfy the masses, I figured I should keep cooking.

~~~~~~

FRUSTRATED—OPEN-FACED SWORDFISH WITH ARUGULA AND JALAPEÑO CITRUS DRESSING

This open-faced sandwich is much simpler than it seems. Fish, seasoned with cilantro and parsley, is mixed with Eric Ripert's jalapeño emulsion from his On the Line *cookbook.*

Jalapeño emulsion (recipe below)
1 yellow bell pepper
2 tablespoons olive oil
1 tablespoon lemon juice
1 tablespoon minced shallot
½ tablespoon mustard
salt and pepper
2 cups arugula leaves
2 swordfish steaks, about 6 ounces each
1 teaspoon cayenne pepper
1 tablespoon chopped fresh cilantro
1 tablespoon chopped fresh parsley
1 teaspoon cumin
2 tablespoons vegetable oil
2 slices crusty Italian bread

Jalapeño emulsion
3 jalapeños, chopped
¼ cup fresh cilantro leaves

1 teaspoon chopped shallot
juice of 1 lemon (about ¼ cup)
¼ cup chopped cucumber
6 tablespoons olive oil
sea salt
ground white pepper

For the emulsion: Place the jalapeños, cilantro, shallot, lemon juice, cucumber, and oil in a blender and blend until smooth with a consistency slightly thinner than mustard. Season to taste with salt and pepper. Pop in the fridge until ready to use as garnish.

For the roasted pepper: Preheat the oven to 400 degrees. Bake the whole pepper on a baking sheet for 10 minutes, until blackened. Remove and place in a paper bag with a small handful of water sprinkled inside, enough to steam the pepper slightly. Leave inside for 10 minutes, then remove. Scrape or peel off the skin, then slice the yellow pepper into long hearty slices (about 2 inches wide). Set the skinned peppers aside.

Mix the olive oil, lemon juice, shallot, mustard, and salt and pepper in a small bowl and gently toss the arugula in the mixture to coat the leaves.

Season the swordfish with salt and black pepper, cayenne pepper, cilantro, parsley, and cumin. Warm the vegetable oil in a medium nonstick pan on medium-high heat and cook the swordfish 2 to 4 minutes on each side.

Toast the bread. Spread each slice of bread with about half of the jalapeño emulsion, then add the dressed greens, swordfish, and roasted pepper, and top with more emulsion. Makes 2 open-faced sandwiches.

sandwich

#19

WORKING LATE—PRIME RIB STEAK SANDWICH WITH CARAMELIZED ONIONS

Here's another sandwich that seemed complicated at the time, but it's mostly a matter of seasoning the meat properly, caramelizing some onions, and using some nice sturdy rolls. To this day, this remains one of E's favorites.

1 medium onion
5 tablespoons unsalted butter (for cooking and buttering bread)
1 pound prime rib, cut into 4 steaks
2 tablespoons chopped fresh rosemary
2 tablespoons chopped fresh thyme
2 tablespoons black pepper
kosher salt
2 medium ciabatta rolls or hearty sandwich buns, halved
2 tablespoons thick seeded mustard
1 cup arugula leaves
3 tablespoons olive oil

Caramelize the onions first, since they take about 30 minutes to cook. Cut the onion into thick slices, and place in a nonstick pan on medium heat with about 2 tablespoons of butter (or you can start with 1 tablespoon and add another later, as the onions cook down, so they don't stick). Let them cook down until brown, stirring frequently so they don't stick to the pan. Turn the heat down to low after 5 or 10 minutes of cooking. This will help them cook more slowly and evenly. When the onions are brown and clear, remove from heat.

While the onions are cooking, prep the beef. I use a rub of rosemary, thyme, black pepper, and kosher salt, but feel free to use whatever seasonings you like. Sprinkle with kosher salt, then rub the thyme, rosemary, and black pepper over both sides of each steak. Heat a large nonstick pan over medium heat. Once the pan is hot, add 1 tablespoon of olive oil and sear steaks on one side. Flip the steaks once, halfway through cooking. Then add 2 tablespoons of butter to the pan. Slightly tilt the pan toward you, and baste continuously by spooning the butter and olive oil over the steak. Steaks are done once the inside of the meat reaches around 120 degrees (for rare steak)—about 4 to 5 minutes.

Let the meat rest for 10 minutes, then slice it thin, cutting across the grain. Spread butter on the buns and toast for about 4 minutes in oven or toaster, until medium dark. Spread mustard on both sides of the rolls. In a small bowl, gently toss the arugula in the remaining olive oil, salt, and pepper to coat the leaves, and place on the bottoms of the rolls. Divide steak slices evenly among the sandwiches and top with caramelized onions. Finish with the top halves of the rolls. Cut in half if you like. Makes 2 large or 4 small sandwiches.

FALL DINNER PARTY—BACON, ARUGULA, AND MANCHEGO CHEESE PANINI

3 or 4 strips of bacon
1 tablespoon unsalted butter
2 oversize slices bread
¾ cup arugula leaves
1 tablespoon chopped fresh basil
1 tablespoon olive oil
salt and pepper
3 or 4 thin slices Manchego cheese

Cook the bacon until crisp, then place it on a paper-towel-lined plate or cooling rack to drain off oil. Butter both slices of bread. In a small bowl, lightly toss the arugula and basil with olive oil, salt, and pepper to coat the leaves. On the bottom piece, lay some of the Manchego cheese, the bacon, and the arugula. Top with a few more very thin slices of Manchego. Finish with the top piece of bread.

If using a panini press, place sandwich in machine and toast until bread is browned and cheese is melted. If using stovetop, put the panini in a nonstick pan on medium-high heat and place a sandwich or meat press on top so it heats evenly throughout. Toast 2 to 3 minutes on each side, turning once carefully. Remove from pan and cut in half or in sections with a serrated knife. Makes 1 large sandwich or 4 mini-sandwiches.

FALL DINNER PARTY PART 2—CARAMELIZED ONION, MOZZARELLA, AND BASIL PANINI

I served this one along with #34 (see page 55) for friends at a dinner party. So gooey and rich, I recommend cutting this one into quarters and serving as party appetizers or a snack for 2 or 3 people.

3 tablespoons unsalted butter
1 medium onion, cut into thick slices
pinch of salt
pinch of sugar (optional)
1 cup arugula leaves
2 to 3 tablespoons olive oil
black pepper
2 oversize slices bread
3 or 4 slices mozzarella cheese
¼ cup chopped fresh basil

Caramelize the onion: Heat the butter in a large nonstick pan on medium heat. Add the onion slices and cook slowly over medium heat until translucent. Add a pinch of salt halfway through, and sugar if you wish. Stir frequently—every minute or two—so they don't burn, but cook until the onions are brown like almonds or walnuts. Cooking time will likely take about 30 to 40 minutes. Set aside.

In a small bowl, lightly toss the arugula with 2 tablespoons of olive oil and pepper to coat the leaves. Drizzle olive oil on both pieces of bread. On the bottom piece, lay some of the mozzarella cheese, then caramelized onion. Add the arugula. Sprinkle the basil on top, then lay on a few more slices of mozzarella. Finish with the other piece of bread, and drizzle more olive oil on top to give the bread color when it toasts.

Put the panini in a nonstick pan on medium-high heat. Place a sandwich or meat press on top so it heats evenly throughout. Toast 2 to 3 minutes on each side, turning once carefully. (Or see instructions for using a panini press, page 55.) Remove from pan and cut in half or in sections with a serrated knife. Makes 1 large sandwich or 4 mini-sandwiches.

SIX

Sandwiches were everything to my second-grade self. They were lunch. They were currency. A token of mother's love. A membership card to the cool kids' table at the school cafeteria.

If your sandwich had toasted bread, cut into two perfect halves with the crusts trimmed off? You felt like the favorite child. Greasy white bread, wilted lettuce, and mayo, no mustard? "Are you an orphan?" the kids at school would ask.

Sandwiches were bargaining chips—if a kid wanted a better seat in the cafeteria, or wished to strike up a conversation with his playground crush, he could swap his crisp turkey and cheese for his classmate's soggy peanut butter and grape jelly. One sandwich could serve as nourishment and a note of affection.

My mother had always looked younger than the other moms, even though they were the same age, staving off wrinkles and gray hair well past my school years. Her deep brown eyes bore down on you intensely, like a cat's, but her laugh was disarming, flirtatious, even. Her warm, chatty personality made her popular with the cable guy, the grocery store clerks, and all the boys in my seventh-grade class—they all had major crushes on her. More important, she was a devoted wife and mother who made more than a few sandwiches in her day.

Packing my lunch was the first thing Mom did every morning. She carefully assembled my sandwich and coupled it with a piece of fruit. For dessert, she included Twinkies or Ho Hos—it was the '80s—and a juice box in a brown paper bag with my name scrawled on the front. Another sign I was loved: She took the time to Picasso up my sandwich bag with doodles of little flowers or birds or figurines. She also included little notes with them: "I love you" or "Have a great day."

When lunch boxes were the cool thing to carry, I had one. I remember carrying a red Rainbow Brite lunch pail around first grade. And a pink My Little Pony one. Later, I toted a Holly Hobby powder-blue tin box.

Sandwiches for me varied from turkey and Swiss to chipped beef with cream cheese. I remember one six-month period when I exclusively ate sandwiches on rye bread. Even the peanut butter and jelly ones, which, by the way, NEVER had grape jelly because grape jelly was the absolute worst—it was a step above mixing gelatin with grape Kool-Aid. Not one real grape is used. (For a grown-up take on PB&J, see pages 66-70.)

Then there was the Marshmallow Fluff phase. I discovered Marshmallow Fluff in second grade, on the lower shelf in aisle 4 at Jewel-Osco. The stuff was designed to be a convenience food—if you simply cannot find time to melt marshmallows, get Marshmallow Fluff. "I used to have these fluffernutter sandwiches all the time," Mom said, and made mine with an even spread of creamy peanut butter on one piece of bread, marshmallow on the other. They were, essentially, dessert. I eventually made them for myself, packing the marshmallow twice as thick as the peanut butter on English muffins. It's no surprise I was a chunky middle-schooler.

sandwich

#46

PHEASANT SLIDERS

My dad has always been a hunter, and pheasant is something he shot during hunting season. It's a thin bird with little fat to hold flavor, so add some by brining the bird for a few hours and layering bacon on during cooking.

1 whole pheasant, thawed

water to cover pheasant

2 teaspoons salt

2 teaspoons sugar

1 lemon, sliced

handful fresh thyme sprigs (about ¼ cup)

3 cloves garlic, sliced

3 bay leaves

salt and pepper

½ medium orange

½ medium onion

4 or 5 strips bacon

4 small rolls

1 tablespoon unsalted butter

1 cup mixed salad greens

1 tablespoon olive oil

Shotgun sauce
3 or 4 tablespoons unsalted butter
1 jar (8 ounces) red currant jelly
2 to 3 teaspoons Worcestershire sauce
salt and pepper

Brine the bird in salt water, sugar, lemon, sprigs of thyme, garlic, and bay leaves for 4 to 6 hours. (Honestly, we brined ours for 1 hour; we were short on time. Tasted just as juicy, in my opinion.)

Preheat the oven to 350 degrees. Remove the bird from the brine and rub with salt and pepper. Gently squeeze the cut orange so juice runs over. Then insert the same half-orange into the bird's cavity. Halve the onion and place both pieces in the bird. Wrap the entire bird in strips of bacon. Tie the strips of bacon to the bird with twine. (Think of tying a mattress to the top of your Jeep. Same premise.)

In a medium nonstick pan on medium-high heat with a pat of butter, brown the bird on all sides (5 minutes altogether) before placing it in the oven.

After 20 minutes, take off the bacon. Continue cooking the pheasant for another 30 minutes or so, basting frequently. Total cooking time for the bird is about 1 hour. When taking the bird out of the oven, turn it upside down on the cutting board and allow to rest for 15 minutes. Carve.

Make your shotgun sauce: In a saucepan over medium heat, melt the butter and add the red currant jelly until you get the proper consistency—thin enough to pour but thick enough to coat the back of a spoon. Add 2 teaspoons Worcestershire sauce, and salt and pepper to taste.

Assemble sandwiches with the bottom bun, then dressed greens (olive oil and black pepper), then pheasant. Dollop on shotgun sauce. Finish with the top bun. Makes 4 small sandwiches.

sandwich

#179

NOT YOUR MOTHER'S ROAST BEEF—SPICY FRENCH DIP

One of my mother's specialties was roast beef. Hers was roasted in the oven and came out needing gravy. But I roasted mine in the Crock-Pot, and it came out juicier and more tender. Sorry, Mom!

2 to 3 pounds bottom round roast
1 medium onion, sliced
1¼ cups beef broth
½ cup balsamic vinegar
1 tablespoon smoked paprika
1 tablespoon soy sauce
1 tablespoon Worcestershire sauce
1 teaspoon red pepper flakes
1½ tablespoons tomato mix (or about one teaspoon each of dried parsley and sun-dried tomato flakes)
3 garlic cloves
salt and pepper
2 or 3 jalapeño slices (optional)
4 to 6 challah rolls

Place the roast in a Crock-Pot with the sliced onion. In a small bowl, combine the beef broth, balsamic vinegar, smoked paprika, soy sauce, Worcestershire sauce, red pepper flakes, tomato mix, garlic, salt, and pepper, and pour the sauce all over the meat. Cook for 6 hours on medium heat or 4 hours on high heat.

When the meat is finished, place in a large dish and shred into small pieces with a knife and fork. Take the remaining juice, strain through a sieve into a bowl, and, if necessary, skim any fat off the top. Add two or three jalapeño slices into the jus for an extra spicy kick.

Scoop the meat onto the buns, and serve jus in a small dish or bowl for dipping. Makes 4 to 6 sandwiches.

sandwich

#28

MY REUBEN SANDWICH

Reuben sandwiches were also one of Mom's best. When I made one for E, I made sure to use good, hearty rye bread, just like from the six months of rye-bread-only sandwiches in grade school I so fondly remember. Toasting it all in a nonstick pan will melt the Swiss cheese nicely.

2 tablespoons unsalted butter
4 slices rye bread
2 tablespoons Dijon-style mustard (such as Grey Poupon)
4 slices Swiss cheese
4 slices corned beef or pastrami
½ cup sauerkraut
salt and pepper

Butter one side of each piece of bread. Flip the slices over and spread with mustard. On the bottom pieces of bread, lay slices of Swiss cheese, then corned beef. Spoon out the sauerkraut and smooth a thick layer over the meat. Top with another thin layer of Swiss cheese. Finish with the other slices of bread, mustard side down.

Toast each sandwich on medium-high heat in a nonstick pan or grill it in the oven until cheese melts and the bread is crispy. Flip it once. Place the sandwich back in the pan. Toast the other side. Serve while it's still hot. Makes 2 sandwiches.

LIKE PEANUT BUTTER AND JELLY

E and I had a whole debate over peanut butter in aisle 5 at Fairway one day. I like Skippy's reduced-fat creamy (it has a mealy texture that I like) and E is a Jif chunky guy. We ended up buying jars of both to keep peace in the kitchen.

I did eight versions of PB&J by the end of the project. Here are six favorites.

PEANUT BUTTER, APRICOT, AND CHOCOLATE HOT PRESS

Brown this in a nonstick pan until the bread is crusted brown and the chocolate melts, and this sandwich tastes just like a doughnut.

**2 slices bread
2 teaspoons peanut butter
2 teaspoons apricot jam
1 small handful semi-sweet chocolate chips
1 tablespoon unsalted butter
sprinkle of confectioners' sugar (optional)**

Spread peanut butter on one slice of bread. Spread apricot jam on the other slice. Sprinkle the chocolate chips on the peanut butter. Top the peanut-butter-and-chocolate piece of bread with the apricot-jam piece. Melt the butter over medium heat in a nonstick pan, then place the sandwich in the pan and hold in place with a sandwich press. After 2 minutes or so, flip the sandwich and toast the other side. Sprinkle with confectioners' sugar if desired. Remove from heat and cut into halves. Makes 1 sandwich. Share with someone else. Please. Or else risk gaining 5 pounds.

PEANUT BUTTER WITH APPLE BUTTER /
HONEY ALMOND BUTTER AND RED CURRANT JAM

I wanted to commemorate sandwich #100 with whatever special sandwich E wanted. You know what he picked? The good ol' peanut butter and jelly. Different nut butters and flavors of jam provide variations on the classic PB&J.

4 slices bread
1 heaping tablespoon peanut butter
1 heaping tablespoon apple butter
1 heaping tablespoon honey almond butter
1 tablespoon red currant jam

Toast the bread. Spread peanut butter on one slice of bread. Spread apple butter on another. Close the sandwich. Then, spread honey almond butter on one slice of bread, and red currant jam on another. Close the sandwich. Cut both sandwiches in half. Makes 2 different sandwiches.

#160 AND 161

ELVIS SANDWICH, TWO WAYS

Halfway through the 300, people would say, "You better hurry up if you ever want to get engaged." I didn't see anyone volunteering to help me cook! And why should I hurry up? Nevertheless, I made two versions of the Elvis sandwich at once in a futile effort to "speed" things up.

4 or 5 strips bacon
4 slices bread
2 tablespoons peanut butter
2 tablespoons almond butter
1 banana, sliced
1 pear, sliced
1 tablespoon honey

Cook bacon to desired crispness. Toast the bread. Smooth peanut butter on one slice of bread, almond butter on another. Lay sliced banana on the peanut butter, and sliced pear on the almond butter. Layer bacon strips on both. Drizzle both with honey. Close both sandwiches with another piece of bread. Cut in half. Makes 2 different sandwiches. Try not to sing "Don't Be Cruel" as you chew.

sandwich

#245

FRENCH TOAST PEANUT BUTTER AND JELLY

The most decadent of PB&Js. Best eaten for breakfast with a tall glass of milk. Not made for lunch boxes for small kids, unless you like seven-year-olds bouncing off your chandeliers. In that case, proceed!

3 eggs
3 tablespoons sweetened condensed milk
1 tablespoon cinnamon
1 tablespoon nutmeg
1 tablespoon unsalted butter
2 slices bread
1 tablespoon peanut butter
1 tablespoon jam (for this one, I used peach)

In a large bowl, whisk together the eggs, condensed milk, cinnamon, and nutmeg. Heat the butter in a large nonstick pan over medium heat. Soak the bread in the egg mixture, letting the excess batter run off. Brown the bread in the pan for a few minutes on each side. Flip once, then remove from heat and let cool. Slather peanut butter on one slice and jam on the other. Close the sandwich and serve. Makes 1 sandwich.

SEVEN

Sundays in Brooklyn are for brunch and lazy strolls through farmer's markets and the ubiquitous specialty shops that line Court Street. One storefront sells fresh mozzarella, another pungent kimchi, the next crisp and chewy artisanal breads that are perfect for piling ingredients on. E and I were just finishing brunch when I got a text from my mom.

> Call me. Dad's in ER.

When I called her back, the world slowed—my father, a smoker for decades, had stage four throat cancer. He had been scheduled for surgery the next week, but the tumor in his throat shifted, causing him to get insufficient oxygen to his brain. "He will need emergency surgery if they can't get oxygen in him, and that surgery may only be 50 percent effective in saving him," my mother said.

My father, the hunter-gatherer, former football player, the loudest man on the block, was about to lose his voice forever, as the only way to save his cancer-stricken life. And it was all happening so fast.

My eyes crossed as I frantically booked a flight home and packed, prepping to stay with my parents for as long as I needed to.

My mother called with updates throughout the day, but none as clear as my father's call to me right before he went in for surgery. "I, lo-o-o-ve—I lo-ve you, Stef. Pra—Pray for Dad, okay?"

And then the phone went dead.

For an hour, E tried to distract me from counting the seconds with comfort food at Supper, our regular Italian joint, and it almost worked . . . almost. I took my first deep breath later that night when my mother texted,

> He made it through surgery.
> He's okay.

I flew home the next day.

When I got to the hospital, my father, weak, thin, smocked in a wispy hospital gown, was silent. He could only communicate with pen and paper. But my father was a fighter, a hunter, a navy man. He accepted the change in his health like a warrior would. He laughed and smiled and cracked jokes, and pulled me tight when I came to hug him. He furiously wrote notes to me to communicate. "How was your flight?" "How is E?" "How is work?" "Can you find me a cheese-burger?"

Dad was transferred to the University of Michigan at Ann Arbor, which had the best doctors for head and neck cancers in the Midwest. The university was a two-hour drive from my parents' house, but only a forty-five-minute drive from E's parents' house. I helped my mother pack up for at least a week's stay at U of M, then drove with her to Ann Arbor.

My mother and I stayed at U of M's on-campus long-stay hotel for families of patients at the hospital. It was basically a dorm room, with no frills, but it had a kitchenette and bathroom, and it was convenient in that you had twenty-four-hour access to your family members because you were right there on campus with them. No worrying about driving when your mind is already scattered from trauma.

I was not dealing with my father's illness well. I had a constant throbbing pain behind my left eye, and I popped Tylenol like candy in hopes of finding some relief physically, if none would be available emotionally. My appetite was nonexistent. I could eat a yogurt and maybe a bagel each day before my stomach succumbed to nervous upset—forget sandwiches! My mother gave me some muscle relaxants to ease my stomach at night so I could sleep. I fainted in the waiting room one afternoon because my blood sugar had dropped after not eating all day. Food was my last priority. My father's health was first.

On Friday, he had surgery to remove most of the cancer. He was groggy and weak when he came out of it, but healthy. His doctors gave a good prognosis after surgery, but it would take time to see how he would heal and to what extent the cancer had spread.

After a week apart, E flew to Michigan and met me in the hospital parking lot with the largest bunch of flowers I'd ever seen. I took E up to my father's room. Dad was weak, and still cloudy from the morphine, but sitting up on his own in a chair next to his hospital bed. I motioned to E. "I'm just going to see if he's awake."

I walked over to my father. "Dad, E is here. I can tell him you're not feeling well if you don't want to meet him."

My father shook his finger, then waved him in.

"Are you sure?"

He nodded yes.

I walked back across the room, and pulled E inside. My mom was sitting on the hospital bed next to my father. E and I walked around the curtain, and my father looked up. He watched as E placed his large vase of flowers on the floor across from the bed. Then E reached out his hand.

I stood in the corner, directly across from my mother. We both watched as my father meandered out of his chair to stand up straight, looking E in the eye, and shake his hand. My mother and I looked at those hands shake up and down, firm and respectful, then looked at each other.

My father slowly sat down, and we all spoke in excited conversation. My father passed notes to E to ask questions about his job, his career, his parents. The mood, for the first time in a week, was re-laxed. Celebratory, even.

After thirty minutes, I walked E out to his car. "Let's go have din-ner at my parents' house," he offered.

"I can't leave my mother here by herself."

"You need a break, and I really want you to meet my parents," E said. "Let me kidnap you."

I had no toothbrush or change of clothes. I had no makeup save for a half-full tube of lip gloss at the bottom of my purse. And I'd been wearing the same clothes for three days. I was not dressed to "meet the parents." But I wanted to. E wanted me to.

E called his mother to tell her we were on our way. "I have noth-ing cooked for dinner," his mother warned.

"That's fine," E said. "We'll order pizza if we need to."

An hour later, we arrived in Grosse Pointe. My headache had less-ened to a dull throbbing by the time we pulled into E's driveway. I was a bit insecure about meeting them for the first time under such dire circumstances, and in the same clothes I'd been sleeping in for days on end. His parents were waiting at the door with open, con-cerned arms. E's father, William, and his mother, Renee, hugged me tightly, then guided me into the kitchen. "You've been through one tough week," she said.

While we kicked off a conversation about my father, my work, E's childhood, and other Grosse Pointe gossip, Renee made a quick chicken salad with pecans and cherries while William poured wine. William is a former record executive. His knowledge of music is en-cyclopedic, from ABBA to ZZ Top, and he has educated his son quite thoroughly on the virtues of *Rolling Stone* and Bob Dylan. He showed me two drawers containing hundreds of perfectly organized CD cases, arranged alphabetically. E and I sat at the bar while I recounted the events of the last week. Wine. Boy, I had forgotten how good wine tasted. They didn't have wine at the dorm-cum-hospital-hotel I was living in.

The salad tasted like a fresh garden, the chicken moist, the cherries sweet, though Renee claimed she "whipped together leftovers." I understood where E got his culinary acumen.

William poured another glass of wine, and another, and all of a sudden it was after midnight and I would be spending the night at my boyfriend's parents' house. When I mentioned that I didn't have a toothbrush, Renee assured me, "There are extras in the bathroom. Help yourself to whatever you need."

I slept in some old shorts and a T-shirt E had in his closet, and passed out in E's childhood bedroom before he finished washing his face and turned out the lights.

The next morning, I came down for breakfast, where a smiling Renee offered coffee. She lovingly poured me a hot mug of brew and flavored it with a bit of orange zest, some cinnamon, and milk frothed with a small handheld immersion blender. To this day, I have never had better home-brewed coffee than hers.

After breakfast, E dropped me back at the hospital, watching as I walked toward my father's room, where my mother was sitting with my frail father. "I'll be there when you get back to New York," he told me.

Over the next week, my father healed. We watched *Monday Night Football* in his hospital room, Dad propped up in bed with his arms crossed over his clipboard and pen, while I sat in the lounger, yelling animatedly when the quarterback fumbled, looking over at Dad. He yelled too, with his arms and facial expressions. It was nonverbal shouting, but shouting nonetheless.

By midweek, we had seen a dozen doctors, nurses, speech pathologists, and others with clipboards and test results. Dad was able to walk around the hospital floor without getting dizzy. Ten days after he'd arrived at U of M, he was discharged.

After a week recuperating at home, my father was stable enough to eat solid foods and walk around. My mother was in control of the situation, able to administer medicine, clean the house, and make dinner. I was confident that Dad was well enough to manage himself. I booked a one-way ticket back home.

E was waiting for me with homemade dinner—fish, with a hearty salad and roasted tomatoes. And wine. And great music. And warm extended arms for me to snuggle in.

It was this experience, this horrible two weeks of my life, and my parents' life, that let me know E was worth making one sandwich for.

Or 300 sandwiches for.

Or, as many sandwiches as he wanted.

sandwich

#30

IN THE QUEUE—CHICKEN SALAD SANDWICH

Friends don't let friends shop while hungry. While waiting in line at Bed Bath & Beyond, stomach growling, I came up with this recipe.

1 rotisserie chicken (use roughly 1 pound of meat)
½ cup chopped celery
½ cup chopped red onion
½ cup mayonnaise (plus 1 optional additional teaspoon for spreading on the croissants)
1½ tablespoons horseradish mustard
1 lemon
1 teaspoon chopped fresh parsley
salt and pepper
4 croissants
4 romaine lettuce leaves

Carve the rotisserie chicken into bite-size pieces. Add the celery and red onion. Add the mayonnaise and horseradish mustard (you can use regular horseradish, though I would use only 1 tablespoon at first, then add more to your desired spiciness). Squeeze the lemon over the mixture (you can add it to taste, but the juice from one lemon should be about right). Add the parsley and season with salt and pepper. Stir until thoroughly mixed.

Lightly toast the croissants, slice them, and spread mayo lightly on each side, if you'd like (this ensures that your salad gets some extra creaminess). Lay a few leaves of romaine on the flatter side of each cut croissant. Spoon salad onto the bed of lettuce. Add more pepper if desired. Finish with the curvier side of the croissant on top. Serve with potato chips. Makes 4 sandwiches.

CHERRY AND PECAN CHICKEN SALAD SANDWICH

Chicken salad with cherries and pecans makes a quick lunch for you or for guests. It's also great for lunch during the work week. Colleagues will be impressed.

1 pound chopped cooked chicken
2 or 3 tablespoons mayonnaise
¼ cup chopped celery
¼ cup dried cherries
¼ cup chopped pecans
juice of ½ lemon
salt and pepper
4 rolls or croissants, sliced
4 to 5 Bibb lettuce leaves

Combine chicken, mayonnaise, celery, cherries, pecans, lemon juice, and salt and pepper in a bowl. On the bottom pieces of bread, lay out lettuce leaves, then top with a generous scoop of chicken salad. Finish with another piece of bread. Makes 4 sandwiches.

EIGHT

My parents said I should stay in New York for Thanksgiving, as my dad healed—I'd be home for Christmas. So instead, we invited E's mom to our apartment and threw a festive dinner party.

Not that I took the lead in the kitchen. Thanksgiving is the decathlon of cooking, and can be pretty daunting to the unseasoned chef—especially this unseasoned chef, who was cooking for her potential mother-in-law and twelve other guests.

By the time I was 100 sandwiches in, there were things I could do well. It was hard to mess up chopped chicken lettuce wraps (#32) or ground turkey burgers (#85). Desserts, like ice cream (#2 and #11) or cookie sandwiches (#50 and #59), were no problem. Grilled cheese (#66, #84, and #86) was a no-brainer.

I even learned to make pesto, which became one of my favorite condiments to whip up for sandwiches.

But I had not roasted a 20-pound turkey on my own. Or made mashed potatoes. And gravy. And stuffing. In one day. For *fifteen people*.

E's mom, Renee, is, as you've gathered by now, a Martha Stewart type of host. She puts out proper serving plates and cloth napkins for regular weeknight dinners. "She gets the table set two days beforehand," E told me of their family's Thanksgiving prep period. I envision Butterball commercials when I think of dinner at their Grosse Pointe home.

Traditions at E's house include watching the Detroit Lions lose their regular Thanksgiving game, a touch of drama, unexpected guests, and a trough of wine. E's mother and grandmother, along with a few helpful relatives, run the show in the kitchen while the men keep to the living room watching football.

E was of the middle generation—he watched football from the kitchen. "You see one Lions loss, you've seen them all. The game is not terribly interesting; we always know how the story ends.

"I was often a kitchen hand," E told me. "I would peel the pears, or cut the veggies. As I got older I prepped side dishes, like salad."

A traditional Thanksgiving at my house also includes football—Dad and I watching the Chicago Bears, if they were playing, or watching the Lions lose—a touch of drama, less wine, but a lot of desserts. Thanksgiving was a two-week process, and Mom ran the show. She shopped two weekends before for the supplies—flour, bread crumbs, piecrusts, sugar, and whatnot—leaving only the veggies and turkey for the week before. Tuesday before Thanksgiving, my mother would start defrosting that bird or tenderizing meats. Wednesday was vegetable prep. After school let out, I'd get in the kitchen and help Mom slice potatoes or make cookies or prepare stuffing. We'd stay up late Wednesday night trying to figure out how to store all the food in a tightly packed refrigerator until the next morning.

On Thursday morning, Mom would rise around 7:00 and begin the rotation of turkey and trimmings into the oven until the turkey was browned like caramel and the mashed potatoes and greens were ready. We had Stove Top stuffing, yams with marshmallows on top, sweet potato pie and pumpkin pie (no, they are not the same). Dinner was served by four, when we'd all pack our plates until there was no white space left on them, and devour the food. Mom could really throw down on holiday meals.

She would also labor over dishes and cleanup for hours, not going to sleep until every last dish or pot was clean, and every single speck was vacuumed up from the dining room carpet, finally collapsing in bed next to my dad after the evening news was off the air. After watching my mother, cooking for the holidays seemed like a daunting task—no matter how good the food or the company was, the host always seemed more exhausted from the day than satisfied from the meal.

For our first Thanksgiving dinner at our apartment, E took over as executive chef because I still wasn't confident enough in the kitchen to host a holiday dinner. He had to man the bird—hell, he had to man the entire menu. I could make a salad. Maybe some sides. But that wasn't enough to feed all our guests! How was I supposed to show I was a decent homemaker in front of E's mom if I couldn't spearhead Thanksgiving dinner?

Just as my mother did, E and I started buying supplies two weeks before Thanksgiving. We had enough serving utensils for about six, but needed service for double the people, plus decorations, serving plates, and groceries. We had different approaches about shopping and prepping a home. E isn't frugal. He is not practical. He buys what he loves, and buys for others what they would love. I'm pragmatic, or, in some cases, downright cheap.

My mother informed me she bought her classic Butterball turkey on sale for 79 cents a pound at her local grocery store in Kalamazoo. In New York, turkeys are more expensive. When E and I walked around the Greenmarket, a guy selling game and meats from a farm upstate took orders for turkeys. I saw the price tag on one he had on hand: $71 for a ten-pound, free-range, organic, grass-fed, Thai-massaged, Botoxed turkey. That was insanity. Later, E told me, "Citarella had 'em for three dollars a pound."

"What?!" I said. "There have to be cheaper ones."

There was, in fact, a frozen turkey on sale at Freshdirect.com for $1.79 a pound. That was about what I figured a New York turkey would cost, given East Coast inflation on the prices of everything.

"No, no, no!" E exclaimed. "Young lady, whatever frozen, genetically modified, pumped-full-of-steroids-and-antibiotics turkey you're used to buying at Costco is absolutely not allowed in this house or on our Thanksgiving table. *Capisce?*"

Okay. Our family and friends were worth the $3-a-pound turkey. Message received.

Next, napkins. Paper works for me. Who needs wrinkle-free re-cycled cloth napkins?

My boyfriend.

E spotted a pair at West Elm he liked, while I spied a cheaper, and admittedly less attractive, set elsewhere.

"Because they're easy to wash? That's their most attractive fea-ture? Yes, let's get those napkins because they're easy to wash," E snipped. "In fact, let's just get a plastic tarp to put down on the kitchen table, huh? That would be even easier!"

We went to Crate and Barrel and bought three beautiful oversize white porcelain serving bowls to serve the stuffing and vegetables. But they were so lovely and shiny, too nice to be used before we pre-sented them on Thanksgiving. I wanted to keep them brand spank-ing new until Thursday, for, as my mom would say, "when company comes over."

One of the worst habits I've picked up from my mother is saving "new stuff" for a special occasion. My mom uses the same 1973 Corelle Old Town Blue and Snowflake Blue patterned dinnerware sets every time I come home. I've seen them at other people's houses, particularly in wood-paneled dining rooms. If you grew up in the '80s, I'm sure you've seen these plates before.

A few years ago, I bought her a brand-new set of white glass plates from Crate and Barrel as a Christmas gift, since my parents had re-built their home in Michigan. They were pretty enough for special occasions, but basic enough for everyday use.

When I went home to visit, arriving from New York usually for holidays or birthdays, the aforementioned "special occasions," I ex-pected she would lay out the new plates I had given her as a gesture of appreciation—similar to making the guest bed with a blanket that your weekend guest gave you, or putting out those Bath & Body Works soaps your friend gave you as a gift when they spend the night. "I don't want to dirty up a whole set of plates," she would say. "I want to keep the others nice and pristine, in case company comes over."

"But I'm company!" I replied.

"No, you're not. You're family!" she said.

Years later, I realized I'm just like my mother with my new stuff. I'll buy a new shirt, but I won't wear it until I have a really special dinner or event to attend, instead of just getting my maximum cost-per-wear out of the item immediately. I even keep the plastic on new electronics until the last minute, so to keep them as "fresh" as possible.

But E couldn't wait to get his hands on the new bowls. As I was leaving for work, E served rich shakshuka with a spicy tomato base in one of the bowls. Breaking one of them in was cute. But when I came home at midnight, I noticed that all three bowls were in the dishwasher, soiled from use.

"Honey, did you HAVE to use the new bowls before company came over?" I said, channeling my mother. "Really? Like there were no other bowls in the house?"

"Save them for what? Are the Obamas coming over?" E replied. "They're paid for, I need a bowl, and so I'm using them."

I sighed. That flash of my mother's brand-new white dishes sitting in the cupboard came across my mind. This notion of saving things for a special occasion is silly. Why not use the pretty plates now, so you have something nice to serve your dinner on, or your favorite snack or cereal or freshly baked chocolate cake or casserole, instead of using the old, chipped plates? Kind of makes each meal—no matter how delicious or fresh—just food.

Life is short! Use the new dishes!

"Besides," E declared, "life *is* a special occasion."

By the time our guests arrived, our apartment had been converted into a safe haven for Thanksgiving orphans. Our barn table had been set for twelve, and a few more gathered at place settings on our kitchen bar.

I watched our friends pile on slices of E's finely brined turkey, my sweet potatoes, Renee's salad, and stuffing and other trimmings. Once everyone stocked their plates, they took seats around the table, on cushions, or at the bar, and the background noise of forks tinkling against our new plates, the chewing of food and contented humming, was music to our ears.

"This turkey is better than my mother's turkey," our friend Amanda said.

"What did you put in the sweet potatoes?" another friend, Shelby, asked. I rattled off the ingredients as if I'd prepared it for years.

"I can't get enough of this stuffing," Jessica, in town from San Francisco, praised.

Our guests were satisfied, titillated even, by the dinner. Some went back for seconds. I was tickled watching how Shelby dug her fork onto our friend Graham's plate to eat his last bit of mashed potatoes. I watched our food that we cooked evoke smiles, laughter, and pleasurable moans. I felt empowered. Yes, getting a killer scoop at Page Six was empowering. Running a marathon was empowering. But watching food you made bring so much happiness to people can strengthen your soul too.

After dinner, some guests splayed out on the couch to watch the end of the football game, others smoked on our patio overlooking downtown Brooklyn. A few took naps. You know you're doing the holidays right when your food is so good people have to sleep it off.

Then we had dessert. Dessert was typically easier for me than a main course because it involves a specific recipe—you follow the instructions to a tee, and it works. You don't and it doesn't. You can't wing it like you can with meat or fish or salads. If you don't add enough baking powder or flour or sugar, your cookies won't rise, your cake will be dry, or your tart will be too damn tart.

A few weeks before we had guests, I baked Oreo cookies from a recipe I found online. Only after I didn't burn them on my first few tries did I feel confident enough to make them for others. I served those up after dinner with whiskey, cognac, and whatever other booze we had left. Booze, incidentally, also helps mask bad cooking. Another solid cooking tip for beginners.

"Dinner turned out fabulous," said Renee. "You and Eric make a good team."

BANANA, WALNUT, RICOTTA, AND HONEY SANDWICH

Need an easy, low-fuss, quick breakfast to make when you're arguing with your honey over napkins? This one is for you.

2 English muffins, halved
2 teaspoons honey
1 banana, sliced
2 tablespoons ricotta cheese
1 teaspoon crushed walnuts
½ teaspoon cinnamon

Toast the English muffins. Drizzle some of the honey on one half of each muffin. Lay some slices of banana on top. Scoop on the ricotta cheese. Lay a few more slices of banana onto the cheese. Sprinkle with crushed walnuts. Drizzle the remaining honey, dust with cinnamon, and finish with the muffin tops. Makes 2 sandwiches.

sandwich

#50

HOMEMADE OREOS

I first made these yummy cookies using a recipe from Brooklyn's Trois Pommes Patisserie that was published on Food Network's website, but I've since tweaked it on my own, after much practice. I prefer cream cheese filling, so I sometimes swap in a cream cheese base for the filling instead of butter and sugar.

Dough
1⅓ cups Dutch-process cocoa powder
1½ cups all-purpose flour, plus more for dusting
¼ teaspoon salt
1 cup (2 sticks) unsalted butter, softened
2 cups granulated sugar
2 large eggs
1 teaspoon vanilla extract

Filling
½ cup (1 stick) unsalted butter, softened
½ cup vegetable shortening
3 cups confectioners' sugar, sifted
1 teaspoon vanilla extract

For the dough: Sift together the cocoa powder, flour, and salt into a small bowl.

In a large bowl, cream the butter and sugar by hand or with a mixer. Add the eggs one at a time, then the vanilla, and mix each ingredient into the dough before adding the next. Add the dry ingredients and mix just until incorporated. Scrape the sides of the bowl with a rubber spatula.

Divide the dough into two pieces. Place one piece between two lightly floured sheets of parchment paper and roll into a ¼-inch-thick rectangle. Repeat with the other piece of dough. Refrigerate both rectangles, covered with the parchment sheets, until firm, at least 1 hour or up to several days. (I actually cooked one piece of the dough, and refrigerated the other to save for Thanksgiving. One section can yield about 12 large cookies.)

Preheat the oven to 325 degrees. Using a round 2-inch cutter, cut the dough into circles. Reroll the scraps and repeat. Place the cookies about 2 inches apart on ungreased baking sheets and chill for 20 minutes.

Bake the cookies until they are set and slightly darker around the edges, about 20 minutes. Cool completely.

For the filling: In a large bowl, cream the butter and shortening until fluffy. Beat in the confectioners' sugar and vanilla.

To make the sandwiches: Flip a cookie upside down and top it with a level tablespoon of filling. Press another cookie on top. Repeat with remaining cookies. Makes 24 large sandwich cookies.

sandwich

#52

THANKSGIVING LEFTOVERS—
TURKEY AND TRIMMINGS SANDWICH

Stack whatever is left of your Thanksgiving leftovers in between two pieces of toasted bread. Serve on the couch and watch the rest of the football game. Pass out until ready for another leftover sandwich.

2 slices bread
2 tablespoons cranberry sauce
2 tablespoons cooked sweet potatoes
2 tablespoons stuffing
2 to 3 romaine lettuce leaves
4 to 5 slices leftover turkey

Toast the bread. On one slice, spread cranberry sauce, then sweet potato, then stuffing. On the other side, lay a bed of lettuce, then pieces of turkey. Carefully place the sweet potato/stuffing side on top of the turkey side. Cut in half and enjoy. Makes 1 sandwich.

sandwiches
95 AND 96

TURKEY AND THREE CHEESE, AND TURKEY AND CRANBERRY SANDWICHES

Two easy versions of turkey paninis right here—one with three of your favorite bitter cheeses, the other with leftover cranberry sauce.

#95

1 tablespoon olive oil
2 slices bread (I used a baguette, sliced into ½-inch-thick pieces)
½ cup shredded cheese (I used a tart three-cheese mix of Asiago, Parmesan, and fontina. Feel free to use whatever you like.)
4 to 5 slices leftover turkey

Drizzle olive oil over the bread slices. Layer shredded cheese on one piece of bread, then turkey slices. Finish with the other piece of bread. Place the sandwich in the panini press and toast until browned. Slice in half. Makes 1 sandwich.

#96

1 tablespoon olive oil
2 slices bread
4 ounces goat cheese, crumbled (about ½ cup)
2 to 3 tablespoons cranberry sauce
4 to 5 slices turkey

Drizzle olive oil over the bread. Layer the goat cheese and cranberry sauce, then the turkey. Place the sandwich in the panini press and toast until browned. Slice in half to serve. Makes 1 sandwich.

sandwich

#202

THE GAME CHANGER—
THANKSGIVING SHOOTER SANDWICH

I asked readers of 300 Sandwiches to send in their best Thanksgiving-leftovers sandwich. This one, hands down, took the cake: the Shooter Sandwich—created in New England, sent in by reader Liz A. Grab whatever leftovers you have in your refrigerator and stuff them into a loaf of white bread. Cover, wrap, squish, cut, and serve.

1 round loaf of really good white bread, unsliced
1 cup leftover mashed potatoes
4 to 5 slices turkey
1 heaping tablespoon of gravy
½ cup or more of stuffing
½ cup crispy shallots or crispy onions
1 cup cranberry sauce
4 or 5 butter lettuce leaves

Cut a "lid" out of your loaf. Hollow out the loaf enough so that your ingredients will fit, but leave a solid wall of bread along the sides to hold everything in.

Layer in your leftovers. You can do it in any order you like, with any leftovers you like. Gravy helps the top stay in place when you replace the "lid."

Put the "lid" back on top. Wrap the sandwich in wax paper and tie around it with twine to keep everything together. Wrap the whole package in foil. Place a sturdy cutting board on top of the sandwich.

STEPHANIE SMITH

Top with a good 10 pounds of weight (cans of pumpkin, bags of flour, cans of condensed milk. Some people grab a dumbbell).

Let it rest under the weights for 3 to 6 hours—you can even leave it overnight. Then, unwrap and cut into triangular wedges. Serve with a side of hot gravy, cranberry sauce, or creamy sweet potatoes. Or plain with a beer or a glass of wine. Makes 8 wedge-shaped sandwiches.

sandwich

#214

APPLE BUTTER EVERYTHING—
TURKEY AND CHEDDAR WITH APPLE BUTTER

We made homemade apple butter in our Crock-Pot (the best housewarming gift we ever received). Apple butter makes a sweet, tasty condiment on toast, and also pairs well with turkey and white cheddar on this sandwich.

1 cup arugula leaves

1 teaspoon apple cider vinegar or olive oil

2 tablespoons apple butter

2 slices bread

2 or 3 slices white cheddar cheese

4 or 5 slices turkey

In a small bowl, lightly toss the arugula in vinegar or olive oil to coat the leaves. Smooth apple butter onto the bottom piece of bread, then layer the cheese, turkey, and greens. Finish with the other piece of bread. Toast the sandwich in a nonstick pan or panini press until it is browned on both sides and the cheese is melted. Cut in half. Makes 1 sandwich.

NINE

My mother did a good Christmas.

The weekend after Thanksgiving, Mom and I would dig out her old cookbooks from the pantry and choose from her most treasured Christmas cookie recipes. She had two cookbooks she used as her main playbooks each year—one from *Better Homes & Gardens,* stuffed with handwritten recipes and newspaper clippings, and a self-assembled one with a laminated cover that I made for her in kindergarten. Each book was a time capsule of Christmas cookies of years past.

Though I didn't thoroughly participate in the Thanksgiving dinner cooking, I loved Christmas cookie baking. I've had a well-developed sweet tooth since an early age, and while helping Mom cut out the cookies with cookie cutters, I licked the bowls to get the extra dough and chocolate. Before the fear of salmonella put an end to this Christmas tradition, I would eat the fresh sweet and salty dough while she baked an assortment of chocolate chip, crescent almond shortbread, and sugar cookies, cut into different shapes and decorated with confectioners' sugar or red and green sprinkles. She always baked enough cookies in one weekend to last us through New Year's Day, and we still had plenty to give to our neighbors in holiday-themed tins.

The first Christmas season E and I spent as a couple in New York, before we moved in together, kicked off several traditions for the two of us. First, we decided to have real Christmas trees, even if they were small and came from the deli around the corner. For our first year, we decided to set up holiday camp at his apartment downtown, since most of the holiday parties we'd go to were below Fourteenth Street. We went together to pick out a strong, thick fir tree from the dozens stacked against the wall of the Korean deli on Second Avenue, where we usually bought toilet paper and Milano cookies at 1:00 A.M. Eighty dollars later we left with a six-foot-tall spruce.

For our first holiday tree, we picked up lights and generic round ornaments from Duane Reade, the drugstore chain. We decorated the tree while listening to Nat King Cole's Christmas carols on Spotify. I thought about my parents' Christmas trees filled with ornaments collected over the years—the ceramic handprint I made for them in kindergarten, the knitted snowflake in second grade. A tree ornament engraved with *Art and Jean,* given to them by my dad's secretary. Their tree was covered in the history of their years as a couple, our years as a family. My history with E was just beginning.

After the tree was up, we hosted a holiday brunch with E's cousin Jane and good friend Laci. E served up scrambled eggs with smoked salmon and black truffles, and played *The Grinch Who Stole Christmas* on his computer. Watching *The Grinch* several times before December 25 would become another of our traditions.

By the next Christmas, E and I were living together and I was about 60 sandwiches into our 300 project. We again had a real tree from the deli, this time one close to our home called Peas and Pickles, which surprisingly had as good a selection as any Vermont forest preserve.

We also hosted our first Annual Holiday Pajama Party, where the dress code required the same sleeping attire you wear at home to wake up and open Christmas gifts in. Robes were also acceptable, so long as guests wore something underneath. Sporting slippers and PJs made more sense than wearing heels and a dress while I cooked and poured drinks.

For the bash, I wore red pajamas I bought from the Victoria's Secret catalogue, figuring if I too bought the PJs, I would be viewed as just as tall, sinewy, and delectably attractive as those Victoria's Secret

Angels. Alas, I was six inches too short and ten pounds heavier than the models, and looked more like a suburban housewife about to tuck into a pint of Ben & Jerry's and a marathon of *The Bachelor*. At least these PJs were fresh, not the comfy ones with the worn-out elastic waistband that no longer snapped into place.

E wore a pair of old flannel PJ bottoms and a T-shirt, and kept his white robe hung up in the bathroom. "I'll be too warm if I cook in a robe," he said.

The PJs idea was genius, if only for this: After all of our guests left, E and I were already dressed to pass out in bed.

We decided to do the party potluck, since we'd cooked a huge feast for the same people just a few weeks prior, but we would handle the Christmas cookies. I didn't have any cookbooks to dig out, but I did have a trusty iPad that I could troll for cookie recipes. I made gingerbread sandwich cookies, shaped like Christmas trees. Pop on a few red and green M&M's for decoration, and the party looked like a real Santa's elf had come over.

People came dressed in their PJs, with wine in hand and Christmas cheer, and stayed at our house while *A Charlie Brown Christmas* played in the background. A singalong to Mariah Carey's "All I Want for Christmas Is You" kicked off, led by me, after a few glasses of eggnog. Two of our friends swapped numbers and ended up going on a date. By the time the party was over, there were very few cookies left.

Of those that were, I packaged up a few and shipped them to my mother so she'd have some while trimming her own Christmas tree with my father in Michigan.

HOLIDAY PARTY—GINGERBREAD COOKIE SANDWICHES

I originally saw this recipe online at TasteofHome.com, but have since adapted the recipe to include cream cheese frosting, which I prefer when I'm baking cookie sandwiches.

[Recipes provided courtesy of Taste of Home magazine. Find more at www.tasteofhome.com.]

Cookies
¾ cup (1½ sticks) unsalted butter, softened
1 cup packed brown sugar
1 egg
¾ cup molasses
4 cups all-purpose flour
3 teaspoons pumpkin pie spice
1½ teaspoons baking soda
1¼ teaspoons ground ginger
¼ teaspoon salt
handful of mini M&M's

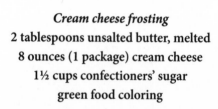

Cream cheese frosting
2 tablespoons unsalted butter, melted
8 ounces (1 package) cream cheese
1½ cups confectioners' sugar
green food coloring

For the cookies: In a large bowl, cream the butter and brown sugar together until light and fluffy. Add the egg and molasses. In a small bowl, combine the flour, pumpkin pie spice, baking soda, ginger, and salt. Gradually add the dry ingredients to the creamed mixture and combine thoroughly. Cover and pop in the fridge for 2 hours or until the dough is easy to handle.

Preheat the oven to 325 degrees. Roll the dough into manageable balls to flatten. On a floured surface, roll the dough into flat, ⅛-inch discs with a rolling pin. (Baker's tip: If you roll the dough between two pieces of parchment paper, the dough won't stick to the rolling pin.) Cut out tree shapes with a cookie cutter and place the cookies on a buttered baking sheet or a sheet lined with parchment paper. On half of the batch, carefully press a few mini M&M's into each cookie (these will be the tops of your sandwiches). Bake for about 10 minutes, until the edges are crisp. Remove from the sheets and let cool on a wire rack.

For the cream cheese frosting: In a bowl, mix the butter, cream cheese, and confectioners' sugar until fluffy and well blended, about 3 minutes. Add a few drops of food coloring until you get the desired shade of Christmas green. Spread frosting on one plain gingerbread tree cookie, and top with an M&M-sprinkled one. Makes about 24 gingerbread sandwiches.

CHICKEN SALAD WITH
CRANBERRIES AND PECANS

A super-easy sandwich to make between all the holiday shopping, gift wrapping, and setting up decor and trimmings for your holiday pajama bash.

1½ cups cubed cooked chicken
¼ cup mayonnaise
¼ cup chopped celery
¼ cup chopped pecans
¼ cup dried cranberries
1 tablespoon chopped shallot
1 tablespoon chopped fresh tarragon
1 lemon wedge
splash of white wine vinegar
salt and pepper
4 slices bread
5 to 6 leaves Boston Bibb lettuce

In a large bowl, combine all the ingredients except the bread and the lettuce.

Toast the bread. Lay lettuce leaves on the bottom slices of bread and scoop chicken salad on top. Finish with another piece of bread. Makes at least 2 sandwiches.

TEN

My father was facing his cancer stoically. But getting sick makes me crazy.

When I get the common cold or flu, I take to bed and try to sleep it off. I don't ask for much from anyone; I just want to pass out, shuffle to the kitchen for juice or a piece of toast, and keep sleeping.

Right after Christmas, I got the flu, a horrible, body-ache-filled, snotty-nosed, high-fever, soul-chilling flu. I stayed imprisoned in my bed, too weak to even meander to the kitchen and stand at the counter long enough to toast bread, and I had a fever so gripping that I sweated through my pajamas at night. Throughout the time that I was a tangled, crampy, sniffling, coughing mess, E tended to me as if I was a princess. He cooked chicken soup, from scratch, with all fresh ingredients, and helped me out of bed to the couch, draping a blanket around my shoulders to help keep me warm. The soup was the only thing that could lure me out of bed on the second day, the hot broth warming my stomach as I sipped. When I was finished, he washed the dishes and cleaned the kitchen while I slinked back to bed. He came to check on me when he was done, but I was already asleep before I could thank him for dinner.

On the third day, my mind cracked. Maybe I was high from the cocktail of drugs I'd been taking, but I became enraged at being sick. I cried hysterically, thinking I was never going to get better. I was delirious with cabin fever, from breathing my own germs for the past few days, wondering if I'd be quarantined in this apartment for life.

You would think the Grim Reaper had knocked on the door and said "You're booked on the 10:15 A.M. flight to hell! Let's go!"

"Really?" E said. "I think you've had too much NyQuil."

By day four, I was back at work, apologizing for being such a hypochondriac, and making a get-out-of-the-doghouse dinner for abusing my nurse boyfriend.

Right around sandwich #70, that Grim Reaper tried finding me again.

There was a lump in my right breast. It was large enough that I could feel it, and it tingled every few hours, reminding me that it was there just when I might have forgotten. "Can you feel it?" I asked E. He could. Probably he wanted an excuse to feel my breasts, but he felt it, nonetheless. I called my gynecologist, and scheduled an appointment for the next day.

My gynecologist sent me to get a mammogram. I'd never had one before. My mother had to get them frequently when she hit her midthirties. She had cysts (was I old enough for those yet?) that often had to be drained, but no breast cancer, thankfully. But my grandmother on my father's side had it, after suffering through colon cancer first.

My mammogram was inconclusive. So was the ultrasound I had immediately after. The radiologist came in to confirm this news in person. "You will need to get a biopsy," she said. "Now, this doesn't mean anything other than we can't tell what it is without taking a sample. It doesn't look like cancer, but we want to make sure. Don't worry."

As soon as the radiologist shut the door, I grew sweaty and flushed, and started softly crying, bending myself into a crumpled ball on the end of the examining table, shivering from both the shock of the lack of information and the crisp air-conditioning. The timeline of my life started to flash before my teary eyes. All of my friends were engaged except me. I was six months away from my thirty-fifth birthday, and 230 sandwiches away from *an engagement ring*! What if I didn't live long enough to see either of those things?

I told E that I needed a biopsy but said it was just a precaution. I didn't want to bring him along and make him worry in case this whole thing was nothing. I also didn't want him to think of my body in a clinical sense. As if something was flawed in it, undesirable, unable to produce babies before we had even planned to have children. He could freak out once there was something to freak out about. Not yet. Hopefully, not ever.

I had to wait five long days for the results of the biopsy. Until then, I paced around the house looking for things to take my mind off it. I made a few sandwiches. I threw myself into work. E took me snowboarding for two days so I could focus on something other than the biopsy results. When we returned, the doctor called. "It's benign," she said. "But you still need a surgeon. We don't really know what it is."

An "atypical vascular breast lesion" is as vague as it sounds. Not cancer, not a cyst, but irregular enough that you should remove it, according to my doctor. She recommended a few surgeons, but through a random connection via a friend of a friend, I ended up seeing a doctor at Memorial Sloan Kettering Cancer Center who specializes in breast surgery in young women. Her team examined me to the hilt, and while they concurred that this lump was definitely not cancer, it certainly didn't need to stay in my body. "I have time on Friday. We can schedule your surgery in the morning." I had forty-eight hours to run errands, notify my editor I'd be out on Friday, and mentally prepare for my first-ever serious surgery. (I had my wisdom teeth out at twelve years old. I was rewarded with McDonald's afterward. This seemed a bit more serious.)

I knew it wasn't cancer, but the anticipation of surgery and a hospital stay still made me nervous. My mind flashed to my father, thinking about what he must go through every time he had to get examined or go to radiation and chemotherapy and have yet another doctor or nurse poke and prod him with needles. I felt the pain for him and wanted to take that pain away. I also didn't want him to have to worry about me while he was worrying about surviving.

E was as relaxed as a Buddha. He cheered that my procedure would take less than an hour. "I'll drive you to the hospital," he said. We nicknamed the lump Lupita, and spoke of it as a freeloading roommate that was being evicted.

The night before my surgery, I came home to a perfectly clean house. Our bed had crisp new sheets and fresh pillows. Candles were burning. E had prepared the perfect post-op sanctuary. Then, E asked a question that cut the tension (and that had been on both of our minds for days): "You think you can get breast implants, since they have to cut 'em open anyway?"

E finds solutions, takes action, and cracks jokes.

At 6:45 A.M., he and I crawled out of bed and drove to the hospital. He parked the car while I checked in, changed into a thin cloth gown, and got settled into my room. A nurse took my vitals. Another one poked the top of my hand, looking for a vein large enough to stick an IV in. I again thought about how many times my father must have had to suffer through this, how many nurses had stuck him with needles, doctors with scalpels, removing more tissue that was once healthy, now dead and useless. I had a flashback to when he was in the hospital. So frail, so dependent on others for food, for care, for transportation. I remembered how much pain he was in. I just wanted him to not suffer anymore.

"Hi, Stephanie, I'm a nurse here working with the doctor. I'm going to take your blood pressure."

"Okay," I mumbled. It was 138 over 60. High for me.

"Are you nervous?"

"Yes, I don't know why. . . ."

And then I lost it. Tears streamed down my face. I had to cover my eyes with my hands. E leaned over. "Are you okay?" He reached for a tissue.

"Honey, what's wrong?"

"I'm just so . . . I don't."

"Are you scared?"

"Yes."

"That's normal," the nurse said. "Surgery is scary. But you know you are going to be fine, right? What you have is not cancer."

"I know," I replied, "but my father does."

"Oh, I'm sorry, I had no idea. Is he sick now?"

"Yes."

"I'm sorry, is he in the hospital or home?"

"He's home. But I just . . . feel guilty."

"Guilty about what?"

It was the transfer of pain from my father to myself. I could feel his pain, the anxiety he must have about going to the hospital after years of tests and procedures.

"Just sitting here in a hospital bed and having surgery, I sympathize with what he must have had to go through over the past year. And I just got . . ."

"Emotional," the nurse finished.

"Yes."

"Well, honey, he's okay and you're okay. You're going to be fine. I promise you."

I calmed down, and E took my hand in his. "I didn't know you were that upset about your father."

"I tried not to burden you with it. But it bothers me. Still."

He leaned over and hugged me. Then he tucked me into the bed, pulling the covers over me tightly, and propping the pillow up. "Relax before the surgery. You're going to be fine."

I cuddled up underneath the blanket, still holding E's hand, and closed my eyes. The hum of the hospital and the TV perched on the wall helped me drift off to sleep.

I didn't wake up until a nurse announced that the doctor was ready for me. "Let's head down to the operating room. Can you walk?"

"Yes."

I gingerly got out of bed and walked into the hallway. I gave E a big hug. He squeezed me tight and kissed me on the forehead. "I'll be waiting for you in the recovery room."

I winked at him, turned, and walked toward the double doors at the end of the hall.

Now, I don't know if this happens in all operating rooms, and I'm not sure my father had this in his, but in my operating room, the mood was festive. After I put on my shower cap and booties, the doors were thrown open to the OR, and simultaneously, I heard that unmistakable opening riff to Michael Jackson's "Don't Stop Till You Get Enough."

It was so surprising, I stared at my nurse, and started waving my hands like I just didn't care. "Dance Party!!!!" I beamed.

"All right!" said the tech behind the computer, and the four of us danced around until the first verse kicked in. Then I lay down on the table, smiled, and promptly fell into an anesthesia-induced sleep.

After the surgery, I woke up groggy but otherwise healthy and happy and not even that sore. Everything was fine. I've felt more pain after popping a zit. I slept for twenty-four hours, and then shuffled from couch to kitchen and back through the weekend. E made me some great meals—a homemade chicken soup the first night, a light tuna steak the next. I was back on my feet by Sunday, making versions of hummus, in honor of Lupita. She was about the size of two chickpeas fused together. And she no longer lived in my chest.

A few weeks later, I got the final results from my doctor about Lupita, the benign yet atypical mass. Turns out, the mass was so atypical, only one other woman in the history of modern breast medicine is documented in medical research as having one treated. Talk about one (or two) in a million.

My doctor told me my special case would likely be discussed at an upcoming medical conference since it was so rare. "Congratulations," she said, sending me on my way with a hug and a clean bill of health. "I hope I never see you again." Likewise.

E and I picked up duck pastrami and a loaf of Italian bread at our gourmet shop, Foragers, on the way home from work, and made sandwiches for dinner that night, with herbed goat cheese and honey.

After dinner, we craved hot chocolate, but we ran out of milk. It was a bone-chilling ten degrees outside. "I'll go to the store," E volunteered without any hesitation. While I cleaned the kitchen and settled to work at my computer, E sprinted to the liquor store and the deli, made the drinks, and walked into our home office, where I was plugging away at the blog, with two steaming mugs of hot chocolate spiked with Baileys Irish Cream. He sat his mug next to mine on the desk and smiled, extremely grateful, as was I, that Lupita was a distant memory.

sandwich

74

RARE BIRD—DUCK PASTRAMI
WITH GOAT CHEESE AND HONEY

*Duck pastrami can be found at most gourmet grocery stores. E will make his
own on occasion, but you'll need to plan a week in advance if you want to
have cold cuts for lunch.*

1 roll
2 tablespoons spicy mustard
1 to 2 heaping tablespoons goat cheese
1 teaspoon honey
4 to 6 slices duck pastrami
4 to 5 leaves lettuce

Slice and toast the roll. Spread mustard on both sides, then smear
goat cheese on both sides and drizzle honey over the goat cheese.
Layer pastrami on one side. Cover the meat with lettuce. Close the
sandwich with the other half of the roll. Makes 1 sandwich.

PUMPKIN HUMMUS WITH GREEK YOGURT

I made three versions of hummus while I was recovering from surgery—a plain version, a peanut butter version, and this pumpkin one, which was my favorite. Slather Greek yogurt on it, drizzle a little honey, and it tastes like dessert.

1 large garlic clove, smashed
juice of ½ lemon
1 can (15 ounces) chickpeas, drained
¾ cup pumpkin puree or canned pumpkin
¾ teaspoon dried sage
⅓ teaspoon cinnamon
½ teaspoon salt
3½ tablespoons olive oil
fresh ground pepper to taste
pinch of paprika
1 pita
1 cup plain Greek yogurt
2 or 3 tablespoons honey

Put the garlic, lemon juice, chickpeas, pumpkin, sage, cinnamon, salt, olive oil, pepper, and paprika in a food processor and blend until creamy.

Toast the pita and cut it into quarters. Smear the inside with pumpkin hummus and Greek yogurt, then drizzle the honey. Makes 4 small sandwiches.

sandwich

#84

ON THE MEND—ROASTED TOMATO AND GRILLED CHEDDAR CHEESE

My mother used to always make tomato soup and grilled cheese for me when I was ill. This represents the sandwich version of Mom's homemade cold remedy.

4 small plum-sized tomatoes
1 garlic clove, crushed
2 tablespoons chopped fresh parsley
1 teaspoon sea salt
½ teaspoon cayenne pepper
1 tablespoon black pepper
3 tablespoons olive oil
4 slices bread (I used 1 small baguette, cut into slider-sized sections. Small Italian rolls will also work.)
3 or 4 slices sharp cheddar cheese
3 or 4 fresh basil leaves, chopped
1 tablespoon unsalted butter

Blanch and peel the tomatoes: Have ready a large bowl about half full of ice cubes. Score the skin of each tomato on the bottom with a cross. In a large saucepan, boil enough water to submerge the tomatoes. When the water is boiling, drop in the tomatoes and cook for about 45 seconds, until you see the skins beginning to peel away. Remove the tomatoes with a slotted spoon and immediately place them in the bowl of ice. Once the tomatoes are cool, peel the skins off.

Roast the tomatoes: Preheat the oven to 400 degrees. Cut the peeled tomatoes in half and place them in a shallow oven-safe dish or pan. Sprinkle all over with the garlic, parsley, sea salt, cayenne pepper, and black pepper and generously drizzle olive oil on top, enough to thinly coat the bottom of the dish. Roast the tomatoes for about 30 minutes, rotating the pan from front to back at least once. Remove from oven when the tomatoes are soft and mushy but not blackened.

Lay out the bread. On the bottom pieces, lay slices of cheddar cheese and a tomato or two, and sprinkle basil on top. Finish with the other pieces of bread. Melt the butter in a nonstick pan and on low heat. Place sandwiches in the pan and warm until the cheese melts, 2 to 3 minutes on each side. Flip each sandwich once carefully with a spatula. Makes 2 sandwiches.

ELEVEN

A week later, Lupita-free, I came home late from work after a horrible day at the office. Instead of lashing out at E, I went for wine and conversation with a friend of mine at a midtown bar. I knew that my father was at the doctor's that day. My mother was supposed to call me with an update that afternoon. She never did.

E was waiting for me when I came home.

"I had a crazy day," I spat. "This guy called me at the office and said that he had a great story for me, and turns out it wasn't that great, and then he gets mad at me because I don't want to run the story. And then he cursed me out! I mean, all this over a stupid gossip item about a runaway dog! I mean, who does that?"

"You need to sit down," E said, looking pale.

"Why?"

"I have to tell you something important."

We sat close together on the couch. E grabbed my hands and searched for the proper words to explain whatever he needed to explain. He looked as if he was about to cry.

"Your mother called me today. She didn't want to call you at work because she wanted you to be at home when you found this out. So she told me to tell you."

He took a breath.

"Your father went to the doctor today. They told him he only has six to nine months to live."

I sat there motionless. I could feel E's arms around me, but the inside of my body felt hollow, as if I had no organs or muscles. I knew my father was ill. I didn't know he was that ill.

For the last year, I'd been on pins and needles hoping this day wouldn't come. The day when we'd have to prep for his good-bye. The last of everything—the last birthdays, Christmases, holidays, vacations. This call.

"Honey, are you okay?"

I couldn't speak.

"It's okay if you don't want to talk about it."

I had nothing to say about my father. It's horrifically sad. I had dealt with his diagnosis by celebrating every day that he was here, not dwelling on when he'd be gone. But that night, all of my emotional energy was focused on the man sitting next to me, who didn't ask for this burden of coping with loss, who had it dumped on him by my mother. Our family tragedy did not need to be E's tragedy. Not right now.

"I'm upset that my mother put you in the position to give me this news. Furious."

"No, honey, don't be mad at her. She did what she thought was best. She didn't want to call you at work and upset you when you would be around other people. She thought it best to have you find out from someone else close to you, while you were at home, so you could deal with it then. I'm so sorry, honey. Whatever you need, I'm here for you."

My head hurt thinking about everything. My father. How ill is he? Is he in pain? Is he sad? Is my mother in pain? Is she overwhelmed?

I was overwhelmed.

The tightness around my head, as if a pair of callused hands were grabbing my skull, made my temples pound. I needed my head to stop hurting so I could think about what to do next.

It took me a while to find my breath, but when I did, I exhaled in E's arms. He said, "Your mother is waiting for you. You should call her."

My mother and I spoke for half an hour. She sounded as numb as

I felt. "I'm not sad, because I've been preparing for this for months now. But this is the reality," she said.

And then I jumped ahead to the *what if.*

What if he goes tomorrow? What will my mother do? What will I do?

What if I don't get to see him before I can get home next? What if we don't enjoy another summer on the boat? What if he doesn't see another Christmas?

What if E and I don't get engaged before he goes? Or married? Will my father never meet our children? Will he not be well enough to walk me down the aisle?

Am I a fool for putting our relationship on this timeline that dictated that we can only get engaged after I cook 300 sandwiches for my fiancé-to-be? Am I tempting fate by adhering to this challenge?

What if . . . what if I don't make the sandwiches in time for my father to see E and me be together?

"Come to bed, honey," E called. "Let's get some rest."

Closing my eyes was the only thing I felt I could truly control at that moment.

~~~~~~

ROASTED CHICKEN, TOMATOES,
AND BASIL ON COUNTRY BREAD

When your heart hurts, you want the heartiest things in your kitchen at that particular moment. Find them, and make yourself a sandwich.

<div align="center">

4 or 5 plum-sized vine tomatoes

6 tablespoons olive oil

1 sprig fresh rosemary

½ teaspoon herbes de Provence

2 garlic cloves, minced

salt and pepper

1½ teaspoons mustard

1 teaspoon vinegar

1 cup greens of your choice

2 slices thick country whole wheat or white bread

4 or 5 slices roasted chicken

</div>

Blanch the tomatoes: Have ready a large bowl about half full of ice cubes. Score the skin of each tomato on the bottom with a cross. In a large saucepan, boil enough water to submerge the tomatoes. When the water is boiling, drop in the tomatoes and cook for about 45 seconds, until you see the skins beginning to peel away. Remove the tomatoes with a slotted spoon and immediately place them in the bowl of ice. Once the tomatoes are cool, peel the skins off and cut them in half.

Roast the tomatoes: Preheat oven to 400 degrees. In a small oven-safe dish, drizzle 1½ tablespoons of olive oil. Place the tomatoes (cut side up), rosemary, herbs de Provence, garlic, salt, and pepper, and drizzle with another 1½ tablespoons of olive oil. Roast until soft and juicy, about 40 minutes.

Dress the greens: To make a simple vinaigrette, whisk together ½ teaspoon of mustard and the vinegar in a small bowl. Then slowly add 3 tablespoons of olive oil while constantly whisking to emulsify. Dress the greens in the vinaigrette.

Toast the bread. Slather the remaining mustard on one side of both slices of bread. On the bottom piece of bread, lay the dressed greens, then the chicken, and the roasted tomatoes. Makes 1 sandwich. Slice it in half and share it with someone you love. Then tell them you love them. Every day.

PART TWO

Now We're Cooking!

TWELVE

This is stupid, I thought.

This whole sandwiches-for-a-ring idea is just a waste of time.

My father is dying and if I keep forging ahead making these stupid sandwiches, he won't be around to see me get married. It will take too long! And I would have spent all of this time in the kitchen when I could have been visiting my father, or at least, seducing my hoped-to-be fiancé in other ways to get him to propose.

I was ready to call the whole thing off. Or demand that E propose sooner.

"You can't do that," my mother said on the phone during one of our regular Sunday-afternoon calls. "That's not fair to you or to him. You cannot force the future, or force anyone to marry you."

"But Dad—"

"But nothing," she said, cutting me off. "Focus on one day at a time. Your father is okay today, so be grateful for that. Come home when you can, check in from time to time, and stay strong and happy. When you are strong and happy, the relationship with your man, the one you're living with, can be strong and happy."

It's like when you're sitting on an airplane, and the stewardess tells you to put your oxygen mask on first, and then place the mask on others. "That's how you'll make it to marriage," Mom said.

My father was not one to feel sorry for himself. Sure, he was ill. But as long as he could breathe and walk this earth, he would go about his life to the fullest. He still drove himself to chemo and radiation. He still hung out with his friends. When the weather warmed up, he still went fishing on Lake Michigan, even though his doctors warned against him being on open waters in the hot sun because of the sun's harsh effects on people undergoing chemotherapy and radiation. He still cut two acres of grass every weekend. Cancer be damned.

I wanted to be there every day for him in Michigan, and felt guilty that I was so far away in New York. I called Dad every day to check in, just to say hello or to keep him abreast of what was going on in the world of celebrity. He never complained about his condition, or his symptoms. Instead, he asked about E, about how the sandwich making was going.

Dad sent me regular text messages to check in:

> How many sandwiches did you make this weekend?

or

> I'm going ice fishing today. They would make a nice sandwich—fish, lettuce, cole slaw on a hard roll.

Dad encouraged me to keep making sandwiches instead of worrying about him. "Gotta keep moving," he'd say. So I did.

I kept cooking, as a distraction and a coping mechanism to deal with my father's illness, and in a way, just following Dad's orders. And I picked up the pace a bit, with him in the back of my mind. Maybe I could make it to 300—and E and I would be engaged, maybe married, before he got worse.

Making the first 100 sandwiches was not enjoyable. Sure, my cooking was improving, but it wasn't ... what's the word? ... fun. I thought E and I would do more cooking together, like in those sultry advertisements for olive oil or wine, where the man oversees the meat portion of the meal and the woman helps with the vegetables, and then they meet for a kiss as one pours the other a glass of pinot noir.

Instead E left me to fend for myself. "It's the only way you'll learn," he said.

By sandwich #100, I could have guests over and not panic from having to cook and entertain at once. I cooked steak, chicken, and shrimp for Asian-style buns (numbers #125, #126, and #127) for a quick summer dinner with friends. And instead of burying myself in the kitchen, concentrating so hard on the meat or condiments that I ignored my guests, I could actually make conversation with people as I cooked. Though I'd practiced grilling steak several times after E showed me his trick for keeping it juicy, I was still unsure of my technique, wondering if it was flavorful enough. As I continued to second-guess myself, I grew frustrated. "It's not perfect," I said.

"You see these people in front of you?" E said, pointing to our smiling guests. "They're eating. They're smiling. They're happy. It's all good."

There were no leftovers. Perhaps that steak was perfect.

A WORD ON CONDIMENTS

The things that E found most impressive were not the delectable sandwiches, but my condiments. Homemade condiments can take a sandwich to the next level. A BLT becomes a zingy chipotle crème fraîche BLT; grilled cheese becomes more complex with a zesty pesto or sauce. Below are three of the condiments I use repeatedly on burgers, sandwiches, paninis, and pitas.

FRESH BASIL PESTO

The first homemade condiment that I really truly mastered. Try it with #136, the Italian Burger with Pesto.

2 cups fresh basil
¼ cup pine nuts
2 garlic cloves
⅓ cup grated Parmesan or pecorino Romano cheese
salt and pepper
⅔ cup olive oil
1 lemon wedge

Make the pesto: In a food processor, combine the basil, pine nuts, garlic, cheese, salt, and pepper. Slowly add the olive oil as you blend the ingredients on medium speed. Add the juice from the lemon wedge, and give the pesto one last pulse to make sure it is evenly blended. Yields about 1½ cups.

TOMATO JAM

So much fun to make when you have extra tomatoes left over from the farmer's market. Sugar, apple, and spices make this a tasty spread. Great for #187, the Fall Harvest Beach Break—Sweet Potato, Black Bean, and Corn Burgers.

2 pounds tomatoes, coarsely chopped (ideally heirlooms, but any
tomatoes will do)
¾ cup sugar
1 green apple, chopped
1 teaspoon smoked paprika
½ teaspoon red pepper flakes
1 teaspoon chopped fresh rosemary
½ teaspoon cinnamon
juice from 2 lime wedges
1 teaspoon black pepper

Combine all the ingredients in a large pot. Mix. Bring to a boil, turn down
the heat, and simmer on low heat for 2 hours, stirring frequently. Let cool
before serving or storing in the refrigerator in an airtight glass or plastic
container. Makes about 1 pint.

GINGER CRANBERRY SAUCE

*Great with any of the Thanksgiving leftover sandwiches. Or on its own,
straight from the saucepan.*

12-ounce bag fresh cranberries
½ cup orange juice
½ cup sugar
1 tablespoon freshly grated ginger
½ cup water
1 teaspoon orange zest

Combine all the ingredients in a saucepan, and boil over medium heat until
the berries pop. Stir, skimming off the foam, and let cool. Serve, or refrigerate until ready to use. Makes about 1½ cups.

Pesto is usually made with pine nuts, but they're pricey. I like substituting cashews. Walnuts or peanuts also work well.

4 medium beets, peeled, boiled, and quartered
3 garlic cloves, minced
2 to 3 tablespoons lemon juice
½ cup chopped cashews
½ cup olive oil
¾ cup grated Parmesan cheese
black pepper

In a food processor, pulse the beets quickly to break them down a little before adding the other ingredients. Add the garlic, lemon juice, and cashews, and pulse. Pour in the olive oil, and pulse a few more seconds. Then add Parmesan cheese, ¼ cup at a time for easier blending. Pulse until smooth. Add black pepper to taste and give one last pulse. Serve with toast, crackers, pita, or—naturally—on a sandwich. Makes about 1½ cups.

THIRTEEN

I still made mistakes in the kitchen.

My crab cake sandwiches were abysmal. Ideally you need fresh crabmeat, which I never had time to find after leaving work. The nearest fishmonger was on the west side of Manhattan, and it closed at 7:00 P.M. I usually crawled out of the office closer to 8:00. Fairway had crab legs on display at the fish counter, but they didn't look like they would yield enough meat for crab cakes. I opted for the canned stuff, crossing my fingers it didn't taste like cat food.

My mom's side of the family was from Baltimore, so they make crab cakes like the rest of the country makes hamburgers. My aunt Ann had mastered the recipe. They would get their seafood fresh from a number of crab shacks near the Inner Harbor in downtown Baltimore. Every time we went to visit, my aunt would have a fresh bushel of crabs for the entire house to snack on while we gossiped about what was going on with the cousins and the grandparents. The next day, we'd have crab cakes, fried up hot on the stove, sprinkled with some Tabasco, and served with coleslaw or potato salad. I tried to channel Aunt Ann as I measured out crabmeat, bread crumbs, parsley, lemon juice, and egg into a bowl and formed patties.

Never again—*never again*—will I use canned fish. My crab cakes tasted like trash in Chinatown on a hot summer afternoon. I warned E that we might be ordering from Seamless that night. He still took a few bites, if only to show me he appreciated the effort.

"But, honey, you're making crab cakes," he said. "You would have never tried that a few months ago." True.

Another bad sandwich day: Protein crepes, made with protein powder instead of regular flour, didn't even make it to the frying pan. The mix wouldn't come together, so E and I had to abort the entire meal. Mexican turkey burgers had to be trashed too, after I came home from a cocktail party and was too tipsy to follow the recipe.

One morning, when I was feeling particularly indulgent, I made E a version of muffin breakfast sandwiches—basically muffins cut in half and stuffed with peanut butter and strawberries. On my first attempt to make my own muffins, I used all healthy ingredients—almond flour, applesauce, and honey, versus wheat flour, oil, and sugar. But the muffins didn't rise in the oven and didn't hold together when I took them out of the pan. They looked like crumpled concrete balls, listing over like melting snowmen on a spring day.

"They still taste good," E said after trying one. I chucked them, embarrassed by their lopsided appearance.

The next day, I used regular ol' flour, real eggs, butter, and sugar. They tasted like muffins were supposed to taste. I sliced them in half, stacked strawberries and peanut butter in the middle, and served the muffin sandwiches for breakfast with coffee.

E said it was a badge of honor to say that he'd failed at a meal. "Do you know how many times I had to order pizza for myself because a duck breast didn't turn out the way I planned?" E reassured me. "You can only get better by making mistakes."

My boyfriend's reaction to failures is usually to cover them up with a delicious sauce, or garnish, or dessert. He doesn't curse about the results or stand in the middle of the kitchen and scream, "I FAILED!" like I have done. He will not order takeout unless absolutely necessary. In fact, in the three years we've been dating, he has never ordered takeout once after a failed meal, though he claims he'd done so many times when he first learned to cook.

One thing was becoming increasingly clear to me: I needed to learn to embrace failure. When I first started cooking, I would be so upset by not achieving perfection with each meal. I believed that my ability in the kitchen was directly correlated to my abilities as a girlfriend, successful writer, doting wife, caring mother. I felt if I couldn't properly grill a steak or chop onions, I certainly couldn't take on more complicated challenges. How would I ever make my future child's organic baby food from scratch?

E didn't project his entire manhood through his duck confit (though, if he did, he would be quite the man, because his duck confit is better than I've had at many restaurants in New York). He could start a grease fire in a pan, set off every alarm in our apartment, make a pizza that looks like puke, and still return to the kitchen the next day. If I made a mess in the kitchen, I was often too afraid to cook for a week.

When I made a horrific sloppy Joe for sandwich #10, I didn't try another sloppy Joe for another 100 sandwiches. One hundred! I should have made sloppy Joes the next night, and every night until I got it right. Until those sloppy Joes were gooey and wet and spicy and everything that you see in an ad for Manwich but better. But I was too afraid. I was petrified to look like a fool in the kitchen. Failure, for me, was not fun.

But it was possible to use it as a learning tool, thus making me a better cook.

As I moved along, I let go of the idea of perfection. Cooking isn't perfect. No matter how good you are at it, not every sandwich comes out tasty. Or photogenic. Each meal is an experiment, and not all of them turn out successful.

In fact, if a meal is too programmed, you might as well be eating a prepackaged, frozen TV dinner.

PRACTICE MAKES PERFECT,
SORT OF—BANANA MUFFINS WITH STRAWBERRIES

I tried making these healthy the first time, substituting applesauce for oil, honey for sugar, and almond flour for regular flour. My first batch tasted like foam core. But I got back in the kitchen the next day to make a new batch. I used real sugar and flour, but still replaced the oil with applesauce to cut some of the fat. Besides, is dessert supposed to be healthy?

[Adapted from mybakingaddiction.com]

3 bananas
⅓ cup applesauce
½ cup white sugar
¼ cup light brown sugar
1½ teaspoons vanilla extract
1 egg
1½ cups flour
pinch of salt
¾ tablespoon ground cinnamon
1 teaspoon baking soda
1 teaspoon baking powder
½ cup sliced strawberries

Crumble topping
¼ teaspoon cinnamon
2 tablespoons flour
⅓ cup brown sugar
1 tablespoon unsalted butter, melted

Preheat the oven to 375 degrees. Grease a 12-cup muffin pan, or line each cup with cupcake liners. In a large bowl, mash the bananas. Add the applesauce, sugars, vanilla extract, and egg and combine thoroughly with a whisk or spoon. Set aside.

Sift the flour into a seperate bowl, then add salt, cinnamon, baking soda, and baking powder. Combine the dry ingredients into the wet ingredients until just blended. Pour the mixture into muffin tins.

Mix the crumble topping ingredients in a small bowl, slowly adding the butter and mashing with a fork until you get a crumblike consistency. Sprinkle the mixture on top of the muffins.

Bake for 20 minutes. Remove from oven and let cool before removing muffins from pan.

Slice the muffins in half. Lay slices of strawberries on the bottom muffin halves. Finish with the crumb-topped muffin halves. Makes 9 to 12 fluffy muffin sandwiches.

THE "WORK AND PLAY" BUN SERIES

Buns, served up hot at Asian restaurants around the world, are great for groups. Stuffed with chicken, pork, or vegetables with a bit of teriyaki sauce, they're small enough for snacks but hearty enough for dinner. If you don't make your own steamed buns, you can buy them premade at an Asian market.

HANGER STEAK BUNS

1 pound hanger steak
salt and pepper
1 shallot, chopped
1 cup canola or vegetable oil
6 Asian-style steamed buns
½ cup hoisin sauce
¼ cup chopped fresh cilantro
¼ cup chopped fresh mint
¼ cup chopped peanuts

Season the steak with salt and pepper. In a nonstick pan over medium-low heat, sear the steaks until cooked to desired doneness (we like medium). Remove from heat and let rest.

Fry the shallot in a tall saucepan in the oil over medium-high heat until golden brown, 5 to 10 minutes. Remove from heat and drain on a paper-towel-lined plate.

Steam the buns in a steamer or microwave according to directions on the package. Slather with hoisin sauce.

Slice the meat thin. Hold the buns open with your fingers and place the meat in them. Sprinkle with shallots, cilantro, mint, and chopped peanuts. Makes 6 buns.

sandwich

#126

CHICKEN TERIYAKI BUNS

Slow-cooked teriyaki chicken is great on its own, over rice, or in a sandwich. The simple recipe below, similar to one I found on the popular blog SixSistersStuff.com, is an easy filling for Asian buns.

1 cup chicken broth
½ cup teriyaki sauce
⅓ cup brown sugar
½ teaspoon black pepper
3 garlic cloves, minced
1 pound raw chicken, cut into strips
6 Asian-style steamed buns
¼ cup chopped scallions
½ cup chopped fresh cilantro
¼ cup chopped peanuts
½ cup thinly sliced cucumber

Slow-cook the chicken: In a large bowl, combine the chicken broth, teriyaki sauce, brown sugar, pepper, and garlic. Add the chicken, then pour the whole mixture into your slow cooker. Cook on high for four hours.

Steam the buns in a steamer or microwave according to the directions on the package. Hold them open with your fingers and assemble the buns by scooping some chicken and sauce into each bun, then topping with scallions, cilantro, peanuts, and cucumber. Makes 6 buns.

sandwich

#127

SHRIMP BUNS

1 cup sliced shallots
1 cup canola oil
salt and pepper
8 to 10 tiger prawns (or about 1 pound of shrimp)
pinch of cayenne pepper
2 tablespoons olive oil
3 tablespoons mayonnaise
1 tablespoon Sriracha or other hot sauce
juice from 1 lemon wedge
6 Asian-style steamed buns
½ cup chopped scallions
¼ cup chopped fresh cilantro
½ cup chopped peanuts
½ cup chopped cucumber (optional)
½ cup chopped carrots (optional)

Fry the shallots in a tall saucepan in the canola oil over medium-high heat until golden brown, 5 to 10 minutes. Remove from heat and drain on a paper-towel-lined plate. Season with salt and pepper to taste.

Peel and devein the prawns, and season with salt, black pepper, and cayenne pepper. Warm the olive oil in a large nonstick pan on high heat until the oil smokes. Sear the shrimp for about 1 minute, turning once. Remove from the pan and let cool on a paper-towel-lined plate. Chop into small pieces.

Place the shrimp in a large bowl. Add the mayonnaise and Sriracha.

Squeeze the lemon wedge over the top and mix until well blended. Season to taste with salt and pepper.

Steam the buns in a steamer or microwave according to the directions on the package. Open the buns and scoop shrimp into each. Sprinkle on the shallots, scallions, cilantro, peanuts, cucumber and carrots, or whatever you like. Makes 6 buns.

MOZZARELLA AND HOMEMADE PESTO BLT

One thing I got really good at over time was making pesto. I started with the basics and then moved on to beet pesto (see page 128), or used cashews instead of pine nuts. Below, the basic recipe (see page 126) is used on BLTs for a weekend lunch sandwich. I omitted the raw tomatoes on E's version—raw tomatoes are a Forbidden Food.

5 to 6 strips bacon
1 small bunch arugula (2 to 3 cups)
2 tablespoons olive oil
2 hamburger buns, or baguettes cut into
sandwich-size slices (about 5 inches long)
4 tablespoons fresh basil pesto
½ ball fresh mozzarella (tennis-ball-size), sliced
½ medium tomato, sliced

Fry the bacon to desired crispness in a nonstick pan on medium-low heat. Remove from heat and drain the bacon on a paper-towel-lined plate.

In a small bowl, lightly toss the arugula in olive oil, salt, and pepper to coat the leaves. Toast the baguette (I slice my baguette in half and use top and bottom for sandwiches).

Lay the bread out. Slather pesto on the bottom pieces, then stack the arugula, tomato, mozzarella, a leaf or two of basil, and the bacon. Top with a small dollop of pesto and finish with a piece of bread. Smush gently. Makes 2 sandwiches.

FOURTEEN

I like babies. I planned to have a few eventually—after I got married, established my career, traveled the world, became a fitness model (okay, a pipe dream and overdose of confidence after losing five pounds while training for my first marathon), and had $100K stacked in the bank. By my mid-thirties, I'd spent most of my years trying *not* to get pregnant. In high school, my mother warned me that if I got knocked up before I was married, or at least of adult age, I would be on my own, out on the streets, destitute. No help from Mom and Dad. No college. No future. At sixteen, that was enough to make me terrified even to hold hands with my high school crush.

I made it through high school, then college, then my twenties, without getting pregnant. And thank God—I look back at some of the guys I dated back then and am pretty sure they were in no shape to be fathers, particularly the bartender and the group-sex-loving real estate mogul. But my biological clock started ticking right when I turned thirty-five. At that age, it seemed all of my friends were either pregnant or trying. My friend Jenny was pregnant. My Page Six colleague Ian was prepping for his first child with his wife, Elisa. My Facebook feed was filled with friends posting baby photos of their broods. Celebrities like Megan Fox and Jessica Simpson were constantly photographed at events with their growing bellies, which meant I had to write sappy stories about these glamorous women expecting children with their rich, well-to-do, and ridiculously good-looking fiancés and husbands. I felt the passive-aggressive peer pressure to join the procreating masses.

Yet, at thirty-five, according to statistics, my fertility was waning, while the chances for miscarriages and for birth defects increased. I panicked. This was my first wakeup call that I didn't have all the time in the world to have a kid. My days were numbered. And while I was living with the man I'd love to have kids with, I wasn't married. I wasn't even engaged. Instead, I was 200 or so sandwiches away from even getting engaged, then at least another year away from kids. That put me in my late thirties by the time I had a child. What if it was too late?

E and I had spoken about having children, but it was something we thought of doing after we were married. For him, children were lower on his to-do list than, say, embarking on our next kitesurfing vacation, or creating a new life-changing, venture capital–enticing app. He wanted kids, but not right now.

I went to see a friend of mine, Sue, for lunch. Sue was my "had it all" friend: She had a great job as a top public relations executive at a major fashion magazine, owned a summer house on the Finger Lakes, and was engaged and had her first baby at forty. She worked a solid 8:45 to 6 each day and seemed to have free time to get a weekly manicure and hit a spin class here and there.

Before Sue became a mother and a fiancée, she and I would commiserate often about dating in New York. She finally found her mate, Jim, an entrepreneur, through Match.com. After three months, he asked her to move in. Three months after she had her mail forwarded, she was pregnant. A few weeks after telling me she was pregnant, she was engaged.

We met for lunch one day between our offices near Times Square, making excited conversation about the weather and the news as we waited in line at the trendy salad shop packed with Manhattan's midtown workforce. We found two chairs to sit in facing a Sephora and a Forever 21, and settled into our lunch.

Sue happily sported her engagement ring and showed off pictures of her daughter on her iPhone. While her screen saver was a photo of her fiancé holding their daughter, mine was of the New York skyline.

"So what's going on?" Sue asked. "What sandwich are you on?"

"I'm a hundred and fifty sandwiches away."

"At least you're cooking your ass off. Is that fun?"

"Sometimes," I said. "E and I spend so much more quality time together now. It's good."

"He's a good guy," she seconded.

"But I have been thinking about the timeline."

"You mean until he proposes?"

"Yes."

"Do you think he won't propose?"

"He'd better, after I make him all these damn sandwiches!"

"And the ring better be nice!"

"I know!" I laughed. I stole a glance at Sue's ring as she stabbed at her salad. A pear-shaped, shiny rock the size of my pinky fingernail. "But I'm worried about another timeline. Let's say it takes me another year to finish three hundred sandwiches. Then assume we're still together—as in, we don't kill each other or break up beforehand. Then we're engaged. Then another six months to a year until we're married. Then it's another year until we have a kid. Now I'm in my late thirties, freaking out about my fertility." I took another bite of my salad.

Tourists with fanny packs and children with Mickey Mouse accessories and shopping bags waddled by us as I launched into my theory. "I need to hurry up because we want to get engaged, then in six to nine months get married, then be married for another year and then have kids. But by the time I start having kids I'll be, like, thirty-eight, and maybe it will be too late. What if I become too old to have kids?"

Sue looked at me, fork in mouth, then said, "Look at me. I was forty and it all happened."

"I know, and you're my model of hope for having a baby past thirty-five. But what if I have problems getting pregnant?"

"You're not going to have problems. You're healthy and young. You eat right and exercise."

"I'll never know if I'm going to have problems having kids until I try to start having kids. Which I can't do until we're married."

"Does E want kids?"

"Yes, eventually."

"Have you talked about it?"

"Yes."

"And you both want a family, like soon-ish?"

"Like, not tomorrow, but yes, within the next three years."

"Okay, so by thirty-eight you're having kids. Plenty of time," Sue assured me. She checked her cell phone and a text message of a photo of her daughter from her fiancé came in. Sue smiled and typed a few quick smiley-face emoticons into the reply box. Then she looked up at me. "But, if you want a kid, then why don't you just have a kid?"

"What do you mean, just have a kid?"

"Why do you need to be married? People have kids all the time who aren't married."

I dropped my salad fork into my now empty plastic bowl of greens. I don't know why I hadn't thought of this before.

I don't go to church. I'm not religious, though I am spiritual in an "everything happens for a reason, good things happen to good people" sense. E only believes in the divine power of a good glass of Scotch. We have no religious reason binding us to being married before we have children, other than that was the natural chain of events: "First comes love, then comes marriage, then comes the baby in the baby carriage," is how the song goes, after all.

But this was not the 1950s. No one was going to kick us out of the country club if we had a kid first.

Tons of our friends had had babies without being married. And I don't judge people for doing it that way. But when it came to the ideal way to raise a family for me, I was a traditionalist. I went by the rules of the nursery rhyme. I thought it would be the most ideal situation.

But that timeline exists in a bubble. That was plotting out a life with the perfect mate who was ready to have children at the exact moment I was. With two healthy parents, and grandparents. Where mortality wasn't an issue. When you live anywhere but New York City and can afford to have children and buy a home and have two cars.

Why don't *we just have a kid?* I thought.

"Besides, if you get knocked up first, you get a bigger ring," Sue argued. "Because he'll feel guilty that he got you pregnant, and over-compensate with the diamond!"

I went off birth control immediately after that lunch.

"Maybe we'll just have a kid," I told my mother on the phone during our Sunday Skype session.

"SHHH! Can he *hear you*?!" my mother asked.

"No, he's in the office. I'm in the kitchen."

"Wouldn't you rather be married first?" she asked, careful not to veto the idea entirely. She still wanted grandkids.

"Yes, but—as much as I try—I can't control everything. Life does not work out the way you want all the time. Life can't be planned out to the minute. Besides"—I paused—"I'd like Dad to be able to meet his grandchild. Who knows how much time he has left?"

My mother let out a sigh. "I think you should discuss this with E. See how he feels about children."

"I will, Mom. I'm just saying, why be wedded to the idea of being married first? It's a bit old-fashioned, you know?"

"You're right, people have kids without being married all the time."

"So you wouldn't mind if we had kids first?"

Logic finally settled into my mother's mind. "Do what you want," she sighed. "Just don't ask me to babysit."

. . .

"Why don't we just have a kid?" I asked E over dinner.

Silence.

More silence.

Frowns.

Mouth agape.

Then, a low slow whine.

"Is that the sound of your testicles withdrawing into your body?"

"Yeah."

Maybe we'd wait a year.

TOMATO, MOZZARELLA, AND SCRAMBLED EGG
BREAKFAST SANDWICH

E tended to the herb garden on our balcony, packed with basil, rosemary, thyme, and mint, as if the plants were his children. It gave me good insight as to how he would be as a father. Here I made a simple tomato, mozzarella, and basil sandwich for breakfast with homegrown basil. This was so yummy, E didn't even mind the raw tomato.

4 eggs
2 English muffins, halved
black pepper
1 to 2 teaspoons unsalted butter
3 or 4 slices mozzarella
1 medium tomato, sliced
6 to 8 basil leaves

Scramble the eggs according to desired firmness (E likes 'em runny. See our scrambled egg recipe, page 279). Season with black pepper. Remove from heat.

Toast the English muffins. Slather butter on both sides. On the bottom halves, lay on a slice of mozzarella, then a slice of tomato. Top with 3 to 4 basil leaves. Scoop the warm egg on. Finish with the muffin tops. Makes 2 sandwiches.

CHOCOLATE WHOOPIE PIES WITH
CREAM CHEESE FILLING

I made these, adapted from a recipe I found in Good Housekeeping, when I went to a friend's house to welcome her new baby. They're a great congratulatory gift for a new family. If welcoming a girl to the fray, swap out the blue food coloring for red, and blend a few drops into the cream cheese filling until you get the desired shade of pink.

[Previously published by Good Housekeeping, though this is adapted. Reprinted with permission of Hearst Communications, Inc.]

Cookies
2 cups flour
1 cup sugar
¾ cup milk
6 tablespoons unsalted butter, melted
½ cup unsweetened natural cocoa powder
1 teaspoon baking soda
1 teaspoon vanilla extract
pinch of salt
1 egg

Filling

8 ounces (1 package) cream cheese
½ cup (1 stick) unsalted butter
1 teaspoon vanilla
2½ cups confectioners' sugar
blue food coloring

For the cookies: Preheat the oven to 350 degrees. Line 2 baking sheets with parchment paper. Combine all the ingredients in a large bowl and mix well. Drop dough by ½ teaspoons onto the baking sheets, spacing each spoonful at least 1 inch apart. Pop in the oven for about 15 minutes, until the tops are spongy. Remove from oven and let cool on a baking rack.

Make the filling: Cream cream cheese and butter together in a large bowl. Stir in the vanilla and confectioners' sugar. Slowly add drops of blue food coloring (I recommend spooning a few heaping teaspoons of filling into a small bowl, and adding a drop at a time until you get the desired shade. You can control your dyeing process better that way). Mix well, and set aside.

When the cookies are cool, spread filling with a knife or spoon onto one cookie and top with another. Repeat until all the sandwiches are made. Makes about 24 sandwiches.

SMALL AND SWEET—
GRILLED PEACH AND CREAM CHEESE

Summer reminds me of my mother's peach cobbler, which she still makes for me whenever I am home. I cooked E my first peach cobbler while we were on a romantic (and adventure-packed) vacation in Portland, Oregon, and then tried to re-create a sandwich version of peach cobbler at home. This is a great easy dessert snack for kids if you don't feel like making an entire cobbler for dessert.

2 tablespoons cream cheese
2 slices wheat bread
1 peach, sliced
½ teaspoon cinnamon
½ teaspoon nutmeg
½ teaspoon honey
2 tablespoons unsalted butter

Spread the cream cheese on both slices of the bread. On the bottom piece of bread, lay the peach slices. Sprinkle cinnamon and nutmeg on top. Drizzle with honey. Top with the other piece of bread. Warm the butter in a nonstick pan on medium heat. When the butter has melted, add the sandwich. Press down and toast on each side until browned. Cut in half or quarters. Makes 1 sandwich.

FIFTEEN

Around sandwich #130, just when I was hitting my groove, I lost the will to go on.

I was breaking my neck to make four sandwiches a week for E, plus take beautiful photos and write compelling stories about the sandwiches for my blog. (Not to mention worrying about my dad.) It was as if I had two full-time jobs. Before the project, I spent most nights out at nightclubs and concerts. Now I was spending more nights in—I raced to the grocery store before the meat counter closed to buy chicken or fish. Then I'd shuttle home and experiment with that night's meal and hope that it was good enough to feature on the blog.

And if it was, I needed enough food left over to photograph in daylight, because I learned quickly that taking photographs at night will not yield those lustworthy images, and no, you cannot get the same light by sticking your hamburger under the fluorescent bulbs in the bathroom and against your white shower curtain—which I learned the hard way. My bathroom photo shoot left me with a sandwich that looked like it had been served in a prison cafeteria.

Assuming that the food was good, and I had enough left over, I woke up the next morning at 6:00 and photographed the sandwich on a plate, styled to look somewhat timely to the moment we ate it. But sometimes I didn't have any leftovers, so then I had to get up at 6:00 and grill a whole steak or chicken or smoke a brisket, so that I could photograph it that morning, write a pithy story that went with it, and post it on 300sandwiches.com.

Now, this is also assuming I *had* all of the ingredients for said meal I wanted to photograph at 6:00 in the morning for my food blog. When I didn't, I had to bundle up at 6:45, trudge down to the corner deli that opens at 7:00, and get fruit or flour or bread. But the deli only stocks basic loaf bread. If I was constructing a more complex sandwich, I had to wait another hour and trudge to the gourmet food market, Foragers, a few blocks down and pick up a piping-hot loaf of artisan bread from the selection they get delivered from Tom Cat Bakery or Balthazar in Soho. And then, I'd more times than not see some overpriced gourmet chocolates or yogurts, and pay $25 for a loaf of bread, a yogurt, and chocolate and wonder why the hell I was doing all this in the first place.

I sacrificed my morning yoga at the gym in Brooklyn Heights to make sandwiches for E. I sacrificed blowing out my hair in order to roast vegetables or make grilled fish to assemble sandwiches for my boyfriend. I gave up dropping off clothes at the dry cleaners, all to have more time to cook food for E. All of this, and there were days when he would come rolling out of bed at 8:00, smacking his lips and, one eye open, look at what I was doing and say, "Whatcha got there?"

And I got resentful.

And I wanted to kill him.

I spent an entire summer in the kitchen, experimenting and learning how to cook various foods. I would spend six hours cooking, then another three hours writing or going through photographs, getting my blog in order. Then I realized that I wasn't doing normal Saturday things, like going for brunch with girlfriends or shopping or walking around the West Village.

Maybe I'd been spending too much time in the kitchen. Maybe I'd spent too much time taking care of others and not attending to myself. Despite dating a tall, attractive man who loved me, I didn't feel . . . attractive. I felt tired.

I'd lost that desire to wear heels and put on cute, form-fitting dresses and style my hair, even to have dinner out with E. I'd taken to wearing what was comfortable and throwing my hair in a bun if that's what got me to work/a friend's wedding/drinks out with friends faster and easier. What I wore to bed was even worse. Ratty T-shirts, oversized gray sweatpants, and a set of red cotton PJs that E calls the "red flannel suit." Not exactly Victoria's Secret. More like Santa Claus's Secret.

Poor E. Who'd want to get naked with someone wearing that?

This needed to change. I needed to get my sexy back.

First step: pole dancing class.

My friend Dana, who happens to be quite sexy, thought pole dancing would help me loosen up and express my more seductive self. I'm all for trying new things, so I agreed to meet her at the studio over the weekend where we'd learn to, among other things, "climb and swing" around a pole.

"Stef! I haven't seen you in weeks!" Dana exclaimed. She hadn't seen me much since I started the blog.

"I know, I've been too busy cooking."

I'd known Dana since college. We both pledged Kappa Alpha Theta as sophomores, but both worked two jobs and were hardly around during normal school hours. We developed a friendship over snacks and powwows at all sorts of odd hours in her studio apartment in the attic. Since then, we've bonded over marathon training and healthy eating—in addition to being a lawyer for a major record label, she was a certified Pilates and kettlebell instructor.

She invited me to tag along to strip without stripping. "Let's try it! Can you come with me to Saturday's class?"

I had been a dancer since grade school, and was part of a dance troupe in college that performed at parties and corporate events in Chicago. Dance is why I'm good at coordination sports like badminton and capoeira. I expected pole dancing, at least the athletic choreography of pole dancing, to come naturally to me. "Sure, why not?"

I met Dana at New York Pole Dance, a studio on the fourth floor of a nondescript building in Midtown on the west side. wearing biking shorts and a baggy T-shirt, the attire suggested on the studio website. I was ten minutes early, so I sat in the hallway in front of the studio door just as many other students did. I looked around at my peers, normal-looking girls who were likely secretaries or finance associates. Or dance students, studying tap or ballet, using this class as a fun extracurricular in their studies. All were wearing torn sweatpants or jeans or baggy sweaters in gray or faded blue or pink. None of the girls were overtly sexy, or trying to be overtly sexy. They looked like they were trying to keep warm.

The door to the studio unlocked from the inside, and Ashley, the instructor, a bubbly, muscular woman wearing warm-up pants and a tank top, waved us inside.

I followed Dana to the front desk and settled up for the class, warning Ashley that it was my very first time. "You'll be fine," she said. "Just relax and have fun. There are students of all levels in the class. And don't be frustrated if you cannot climb up the pole the first time."

Climb up the pole? *They teach that in the first class?* I thought.

I popped into the main studio, where the girls who had been sitting outside started to take their places in front of the six poles set up in the studio. One, a small, soft-spoken Asian woman who looked to be no more than twenty years old, had on bike shorts and a custom shredded tank top that exposed a cute hot-pink sports bra underneath. A heavier-set woman with curly red hair set her duffel bag down in the corner. And there was a brown-haired young woman with glasses who stood in the front left corner, wearing a plain white tank top and blue bike shorts. She looked like she studied ballet or tap. Not like she'd swung on a pole at Flashdancers, the self-titled "finest" strip club in New York.

I looked at Dana. She was wearing gold heels, a low-cut bright-colored tank top, and hot-pink shorts that showed off her legs. She wasn't that much better at pole dancing than I was, but she at least looked the part. Dressed as I was, I felt like a schoolmarm next to her.

Ashley strode into the studio, this time wearing bike shorts that showed every muscle in her legs from the ankle to the gluteus maximus (and yes, it was maximus). She cranked on some sultry R&B, Ciara's "Promise," to guide us through the warm-up routine, a series of yoga stretches, abs exercises, and some brief choreography. I had danced to Ciara before, but somehow I felt awkward dancing to the song in front of a large mirror and a pole.

Then we moved to some floor work. "And bottoms up! Two, three, four," the instructor counted off. "Kick that leg, six, seven, eight . . . and weerrkkk, two, three, four . . ."

I writhed around on the floor, trying to feel sexy, but mostly looking around at the other women to see if I looked awkward compared to everyone else. I ran my hands up and down my body as we did ab exercises, and stole a glance over at Dana as we did hip rolls. I felt stiff. When was the last time I ever did this for E? Had I ever?

Then we got to the choreography. Ashley instructed us to stand next to the pole, our left hip jutted out away from it so that our bodies made a half-moon shape outward from it. The stance would help us move around the pole with grace and power, and jump into spins easily. She then counted off a number of paces, then a turn, head shake, bob, twist down, and up. Or something. I got lost at the turn.

"Everyone feel that? Good. Okay, let's take it from the top. Five, six, seven, eight . . ."

I stepped, but I didn't dance. I followed along, but I didn't move around the pole with the same grace as the instructor. My swing, with my leg hooked around the pole, lost power after half a turn. But the quiet Asian girl in the corner glided around the pole like she'd been there before. (Was she a stripper? I wondered.)

Ashley came over to me several times to walk me through the choreography. "Hi, what's your name again?" she asked. "Okay, you've got to, like, feel the music. Be feminine and graceful. Float around the pole. It's not just step step step. It's glide glide, body weight, hips out, then move. Like, *feel* it."

I thought I *was* feeling it.

Then, things really got real. After Ashley taught us the choreography, we took a short break. The other girls in the class fumbled in their duffel bags or oversized totes and pulled out their equipment for the next part of class. Stripper heels. Lucite-soled, five- to six-inch stripper heels.

"Dana, you said we didn't need to bring shoes!"

"You don't," Dana said. "The more experienced girls use shoes. I didn't think in the beginner class students would wear shoes."

So now I couldn't follow the choreography, wasn't wearing the right clothes, and didn't have the proper footwear? My confidence evaporated.

Ashley reappeared, wearing briefs, not bike shorts, and six-inch Lucite heels. She cranked up Aerosmith's "Crazy" and led us through the choreography to the music.

I watched myself in the mirror, without the Lucite heels. I stood awkwardly on my tiptoes to mimic the artificial height the other women gained through their stripper shoes. I moved like a tin can.

Then Ashley taught us how to climb up the pole. Wiggling up took hard-earned athleticism—something weights and Pilates prepped you for. I understood the rules of climbing. Left foot wrapped around the pole, left knee to the outside, right leg wraps around the left, thrust butt out, move up. Change grip, move legs up, repeat. Got that. Barely. But I moved up the pole. And slid down, my legs sticking every few inches. I looked terrified, but I did it.

I had trained for and run two marathons. I had taken eight years of yoga, and years of dance before all of that. I was fit. But I was a clumsy, unathletic dweeb at pole dancing.

The chubby girl to my left exuded more confidence than I did, her body extending and flexing with each movement around the pole. Dana, as much a novice to the class as I was, at least looked sexy in a tank top cut deep on the sides, her neon sports bra visible from underneath. The ballerina, naturally, flipped and swung around the pole effortlessly, light as a ribbon winding her way to the floor.

Ashley instructed us to writhe on the floor, pop up on all fours, and flip our head from one side to the other. Anybody can look sexy if they just fling their hair. Not me. I had my hair in a stiff bun. What the hell? I had lost all sexy. Sexy had left my body.

"Work, girls, yes, sexy!" Ashley called. "Now climb!"

I made my way to the pole, shaking, but able to make it up the pole. "Okay, sexy, now work, bend, snap, swing, and down. Slide sexy! Pretty toes!"

The other girls looked like they could seduce someone, anyone, their boyfriends or men they wanted to be their boyfriends. The ballerina one, who probably took this class as an elective in her four-year dance program at Alvin Ailey or Juilliard, demonstrated Ashley's instructions effortlessly. Even Dana, with her background in Pilates and kettlebells, exuded confidence as she moved. I could not tell this was only her second class.

I felt like the nerd in the back of Chemistry 101 with my Trapper Keeper and glasses.

Compared to the better-coordinated and more alluring students in class, I had as much sex appeal as a rhinoceros. I felt uncoordinated, awkward, stiff, and decidedly not sexy. This scared me. Would E start looking at other women? Would he dump me for a sexy yoga-slash-pole-dancing instructor?!?!

My eyes welled up with tears. As if fumbling my way through heel pivot turns wasn't awkward enough, I then became the fool who cried during pole dancing class.

I kept my face down as I gathered my bags and fled to the changing room. "Did you enjoy it?" Dana asked me.

"*SureyahIjusthavetogetchangediamgoingttoputonmypants,*" I mumbled as I raced by her and the instructor sitting at the front desk.

There I was, at sandwich #130, with chipped nail polish from cooking, with frizzy hair because I spent every weekend making sandwiches instead of getting a cute haircut or funky-colored manicure, in the same free gray T-shirt from Equinox that I'd worn for three years, in an orthopedic sports bra, not exuding any sexiness whatsoever. Even the clothes I changed into—baggy sweater, baggy jeans, flip-flops instead of heels—were for utility, not for showcasing my feminine wiles.

I wiped my face and composed myself enough to pull back the curtain and face the instructor. "How did you like class?" she asked.

"It was okay," I said. "I just didn't think I'd feel so awkward."

"It takes some getting used to. After two classes, you'll get the hang of it. You have the strength to climb the pole and work around it. That's the hard part. But once you get used to the choreography, you'll be fine."

"I hope."

Ashley looked at me. "I think you should sign up for a few more classes. We have a deal going right now. Five classes for the price of three. Your friend just bought that package."

I thought about it. The only way I was going to get better was to practice.

After class, Dana and I walked, then grabbed skim lattes.

"You look upset," she said.

"I can't believe I'm so . . . asexual."

"WHAT?! You're totally sexy."

"I looked at every girl in that room and thought otherwise. They were all feminine and graceful and wear pink and look pretty. When is the last time I even wore heels? Or *pink*?"

I was in tears again. All of those weeks trying to make E happy with sandwiches had left me feeling so overextended, so tethered to the kitchen, that I didn't allow any free time to treat myself—to look at myself outside of my role as chef or cook or maid or caregiver. How was I supposed to be attractive enough for E to want to be with, much less want to stay with, if I didn't love myself?

"Well, how can you start with small things to make yourself feel more attractive?"

"Um . . ." I looked at Dana. "Maybe it comes from wearing sluttier clothes?"

"Ha ha. I don't think you need to dress like a slut to look sexy," she said. "But maybe wearing more overtly feminine clothes, like heels and dresses and bright colors, may help your mood. You know, dress how you want to feel."

"That's a good idea," I said.

"And maybe you should take a break from cooking one weekend."

"But I won't reach my goal in a timely fashion if I don't get cracking . . ."

"Stef, it's okay. Do you really think E won't marry you when he feels ready because you have a hundred and seventy-some sandwiches left?"

"Well, we did make a deal," I said.

At Dana's urging, and for fear of crying at pole dancing class again, I took it upon myself to launch the "sexy back" project.

I vowed to only wear clothes that made me feel pretty—that included sleepwear, which would only be made of silk and lace from now on. I would get weekly manicures and pedicures. I would do my hair every day and not just throw it up haphazardly into a bun (unless that bun was groomed as part of a sexy librarian look). I would make more time to seduce my boyfriend, even if that meant kissing him a hundred times a day. Hell, I might even make sandwiches for E *naked*. Or, at least, wear something while I cook that would want him to get me naked.

That night, I made sweet-and-sour sloppy Joes for dinner. I was craving beef with a spicy tang, just like what I was searching for in myself. Before I hit the kitchen, I got myself glammed up. I put on a cute outfit—shorts and a low-cut top—and enough makeup to look as if I were going on a date. I set the table with wine and candles before we sat down.

Afterward, I told E to draw a bath while I did the dishes, and we cuddled in a soapy tub before we tucked into bed. I put on a black silk nightie instead of the "red flannel suit." I then showed him a few of the snakelike moves I'd learned from sultry Ashley at class. E liked them. A lot. My black nightie soon ended up on our bedroom floor.

As I dozed off to postcoital slumber, I felt more at ease about myself. "I always think you're beautiful," he said. "But you're sexiest when you're confident in yourself."

Dana asked me via text the next day:

> Would you come to pole dancing class again?

"Yes," I said, and signed up for six more classes.

Because, as I'm sure some wise old stripper once said to some young gal just learning to climb and spin, there's no crying in pole dancing. And meanwhile, I had a blog to write.

sandwich

#131

THE SEXY BACK PROJECT—
SWEET-AND-SOUR SLOPPY JOES

I made a sweet-and-sour sloppy Joe with a cabbage salad because that's how I felt at the time—sweet and sour. After failing at my first attempt to make sloppy Joes (sandwich #10), I got this version right, thanks to a recipe I adapted from Real Simple *magazine. Feeling confident in my cooking, I also felt strong enough to go back to pole dancing class the next weekend, where I shimmied up the pole with a smile.*

2 tablespoons olive or canola oil
1 tablespoon minced fresh ginger
1 bunch scallions, chopped
1 pound ground beef
¼ cup soy sauce
3 tablespoons brown sugar
¼ cup tomato sauce
salt and pepper
½ cup water
1 tablespoon red pepper flakes
4 lime wedges
4 hamburger buns, split
½ red cabbage, sliced thin
2 carrots, grated or shredded
½ cup chopped fresh cilantro
2 teaspoons sesame oil

In a large nonstick pan, add 1 tablespoon of olive or canola oil, ginger, and scallions. Soften up the veggies for 2 to 4 minutes on medium heat. Add the beef. Stir and break the meat apart with a wooden spoon. Brown until thoroughly cooked, about 4 minutes. Add the soy sauce, brown sugar, tomato sauce, salt, and pepper to the pan. Add the water and let simmer for another 3 to 4 minutes. Add the red pepper flakes, then add the juice from 1 lime wedge toward the end of cooking.

Brown the buns lightly in the oven at 350 degrees. Remove from oven. Lay out the buns and scoop the filling on.

For the cabbage salad, combine the cabbage, carrots, cilantro, sesame oil, and the remaining olive oil in a bowl and mix. Squeeze the remaining lime wedges on top to add juice, stir a bit more, and serve the salad alongside the sandwiches. Makes 4 sandwiches.

BURGERS, 4 WAYS

Burgers. McDonald's has served billions and billions. I've served . . . four. But they were four good ones, or so I was told by Mr. 300 Sandwiches. Below, burgers four ways, by 300.

sandwich

#49

BURGER WITH EGG

A runny egg on meat? Not my favorite, but for E, I tried it.

1 pound ground beef
1 tablespoon cumin
2 tablespoons chopped red onion
1 tablespoon garlic powder
2 tablespoons chopped fresh parsley
1 tablespoon olive oil
4 eggs
4 hamburger buns
1 tablespoon unsalted butter, melted
handful of greens (about ½ cup)
ketchup, mustard, mayonnaise, salt, and pepper

In a large bowl, combine the beef, cumin, onion, and garlic powder. Add the parsley and olive oil and mix thoroughly enough that all ingredients are blended. Shape into 4 patties. In a nonstick pan, brown on medium heat for about 5 minutes on each side. When the meat is about 80 percent done, in a separate pan, fry 1 egg per sandwich.

Toast the buns. Brush both sides with melted butter. On each bottom half, place greens and then a hamburger patty. Carefully place a fried egg on top of each hamburger. Slather your condiments (ketchup, mustard, mayonnaise, salt, and pepper) on the top halves of the buns and close the sandwiches. Makes 4 burgers.

STEPHANIE SMITH

LAMB BURGER WITH FETA

Lamb burgers were one of the first things I learned to master, along with cereal and caramelized onions. I like them on crusty English muffins with red onion and crème fraîche. Easy dish for backyard barbecues and weekday dinners at home.

½ red onion
¼ cup chopped fresh mint
¼ cup chopped fresh parsley
pinch salt
½ teaspoon cumin
1½ teaspoons paprika
1 pound ground lamb
½ cup feta cheese
2½ tablespoons olive oil
4 English muffins
4 leaves lettuce
⅓ cup crème fraîche

Make the burgers: Mince half of the red onion. In a large bowl, combine the mint, parsley, salt, cumin, half of the paprika, and the minced onion. Add the lamb and cheese. Mix well and add olive oil. Shape into 4 patties. In a large nonstick pan on medium heat, cook the patties about 4 minutes on each side, or until brown. Remove from heat and drain on a paper-towel-lined plate.

Thinly slice the remaining red onion. Toast the English muffins. On the bottom halves, place lettuce and then a lamb burger. Dollop with crème fraîche and small slices of red onion. Finish with the muffin tops and smush down gently. Makes 4 burgers.

sandwich

#136

ITALIAN BURGER WITH PESTO

On this burger, I included roasted tomatoes, mozzarella, and basil to give it an Italian flavor.

2 cups grape tomatoes
¼ cup olive oil
salt and pepper
1 tablespoon herbes de Provence
1 tablespoon cayenne pepper
2 to 3 whole basil leaves (plus more for garnish if desired)
2 tablespoons chopped fresh parsley
2 tablespoons oregano
2 tablespoons Worcestershire sauce
1 pound ground beef
4 hamburger buns
¼ cup pesto (use my recipe from page 126, it's amaze)
1 ball mozzarella, sliced

Fill a small soup pot halfway with water and bring to a boil. Slice an "x" on the top of each tomato with a small knife (this helps you pull off the skin after boiling). Plop tomatoes into boiling water, and remove after a minute. Place them in cold water for a second, then remove. Peel skins off the tomatoes.

Roast the tomatoes: Preheat the oven to 400 degrees. Drizzle a couple tablespoons of the olive oil into a shallow oven-safe dish and place the peeled tomatoes in the dish. Sprinkle with salt, black pepper, herbes de

Provence, and cayenne pepper. Lay the basil leaves on top. Drizzle the remaining olive oil on top, and pop in the oven for about 30 minutes.

Make the burgers: In a large bowl, mix parsley, salt, pepper, oregano, Worcestershire sauce and ground beef. Combine ingredients thoroughly. Shape into 4 patties.

In a medium nonstick pan, cook burgers on medium heat for 3 to 5 minutes on each side, or until desired doneness. Remove and drain on a paper-towel-lined plate.

Remove the tomatoes from the oven. Toast the buns for a minute or two in the oven.

Lay out the buns. Slather pesto on both sides of the buns. On the bottom halves, lay slices of mozzarella and then a hamburger patty. Top each with a heaping spoonful of tomatoes. Garnish with a leaf or two of basil if desired. Finish with the tops of the buns. Makes 4 burgers.

~~~

SWEET POTATO, BLACK BEAN, AND CORN BURGERS
WITH TOMATO JAM

If you have extra veggies left over from a trip to the farmer's market, make this veggie sandwich. I sweetened it all up with homemade tomato jam (page 126) and stacked microgreens on top. A guilt-free burger packed with veggies. All the more reason to pair it with a glass of wine.

1 cup quinoa

2 medium sweet potatoes

1 cup black beans

1 cup corn

¼ cup chopped fresh parsley

1 egg white

¾ cup bread crumbs

1 tablespoon smoked paprika

1 tablespoon cumin

1 teaspoon black pepper

1 tablespoon canola oil

4 hamburger buns

1 cup microgreens

Tomato jam

Cook the quinoa according to directions on the package.

Cook the sweet potatoes: Peel and boil in water for about 10 minutes. Remove from water and, when they have cooled, cut in quarters, place in a food processor and pulse until finely chopped. Place the chopped sweet potatoes in a large bowl with the beans, corn, parsley, cooked quinoa, egg white, bread crumbs, smoked paprika, cumin, and pepper. Shape into 4 burger-size patties, and refrigerate for about ½ hour before cooking, so they firm up and hold their shape.

Pour the canola oil into a large nonstick pan, and warm over medium heat. Cook burgers 4 minutes each side, or until brown, and remove from heat.

Toast the buns. On the bottom halves, lay microgreens, then sweet potato burger, and top with tomato jam. Finish with the tops of the buns. Serve with kale or potato chips. Makes 4 burgers.

SIXTEEN

Text message from Dad:

> Dad: Went to the doctor today for check-up. Everything's OK. What's up with you for the weekend?

> Me: That's good to hear, I need to cook for about 8 hours a day this weekend, and make sandwiches!

> Dad: Just don't eat all the sandwiches. Save some for E. Love you both, take care.

I had no idea that a joke between E and me would end up fascinating millions, confusing some, and getting covered everywhere from *Good Morning Sacramento* to the *Times of India*.

I never wanted to be famous. Never wanted to be a reality star. I don't even like having my picture taken. When I started my blog and forged ahead making sandwiches, I didn't think about what it meant to expose our relationship to anyone who had a computer. I didn't want Internet fame, which is why I kept the blog anonymous. I didn't want to be one of those couples that put our relationship up for public scrutiny for all to judge. I only told friends and family about 300sandwiches.com because I knew they would find the humor in the story. If those people passed it on to their friends, then so be it.

Since I didn't think many people were paying attention, I wrote about our relationship freely, as it related to sandwiches. Sometimes I used it as a place to vent about our sandwich-related fights ("Avocado is a forbidden food!" E said. "But guacamole isn't?" I responded). Or E coming home late after too many Scotches with friends. Or tiffs over who didn't do the dishes. Or the insensitive things we both said to each other, including that I needed to be kept off sugar after 9:00 P.M. because I turned into a gremlin. The blog turned into a diary of sorts, and while I continued to vent to the Internet, believing no one was on the other side, people were reading. People we knew.

My father followed intently. Though the cancer was making him progressively weaker, he was still able to walk around, go shopping, drive himself to appointments, go fishing, and do housework. In between chemo sessions and doctor's appointments, my father sent sandwich suggestions my way to help me reach my goal faster.

"Why don't you do a good liverwurst sandwich?" he asked. My dad was the only person I knew who ate liverwurst. I couldn't go there. E would use that pâté-esque meat in sausage casing as a doorstop.

During football season, Dad encouraged me to make sandwiches for E during the game.

> You should do pulled pork.

Which I did.

No matter how ill he felt from either the cancer or the treatments, he stayed positive, always looking ahead to the day in front of him.

> I am better than yesterday. The sun is out and it's warm, like 50 degrees. Have a great day, love you both.

Love you both, as in E and me. He signed all of his text messages to the both of us, even though I was hundreds of sandwiches away from getting engaged.

The process of writing out what was going on in our relationship actually kept the relationship from suffering from the usual and often unnecessary drama that plagues typical couples. Fights that would have gone unresolved were worked out on the blog before they had time to cause resentment between us.

Once, around sandwich #150, E and I had a raging argument. He'd gotten our brand-new SUV stuck in the sand during a kitesurfing trip, after letting someone else with no insurance drive it as he sailed down the coast. I had told him multiple times not to let anyone else drive the car because if something happens we're liable. But E didn't listen to my (yet again) accurate advice. And I took personal offense at it.

"It started with him coming home super late after a day at the beach with his friends, and then me finding out he got the car stuck in the sand after he let someone else drive it," I wrote on 300 Sandwiches. "It ended with me in tears, screaming, 'I'm tired of feeling like the mom and the maid around here!'"

It's harsh to read about your shortcomings in print, whether it's a job review or the results of a physical at the doctor's office. But reading about our imperfections made us want to correct them quickly. If he said something offensive and read about it on the blog, E apologized profusely. Or, if he had no idea something he said was offensive, and then read my interpretation of it on the blog, we spoke about the incident and worked through it before I hit "publish." Like a half-hour television sitcom, our conflicts were usually resolved within a five-hundred-word blog post.

The drag-out fight about that stupid car was a rare tiff that continued overnight. But the next day, we resolved the problem, or else I would have never continued on with sandwich making:

After things calmed down, we hugged, kissed, said "I'm sorry," and went to brunch to a place that doesn't serve sandwiches. By ourselves. "On the way back, let's get some flowers for the apartment. It will be nice to have something beautiful and living in our kitchen," E said, no doubt secretly thinking "What duct tape can't fix, flowers will."

Instead of posting a photo of a sandwich, I shared a photo of those flowers E bought for me, "to symbolize how just two things sitting alone, just being, in a glass house can be a beautiful thing."

After the post above about the car, I was reminded that my mother was following the blog regularly. She sent this email the next day:

I read your blog. Word to the wise, if you plan to keep this man, you need to tone down your attitude.

These are the things you might do after you get the man, not before. I never did these things before we got married. There is a saying: The same things it took to get him are the same things it takes to keep him. You were nice, kind, and gentle in the beginning. Nobody is going to go into a relationship with someone if they see the bad side first. Don't take this the wrong way, it's just my opinion. I want to see you two make it all the way.

Love you,
Mom

I was aware that my parents were following the blog (after all, I was their child and this was my project and, just like my fifth-grade science project and dance recitals, they were—aside from certain posts—proud of their little girl's work).

But I sometimes forgot that E's parents were also reading. They'd only met me a few times, and here I was exposing our dirty laundry, our romantic interludes, and my thoughts on our relationship to the world. What if they didn't approve of me talking about their son like I do? What if they didn't appreciate me revealing his wearing a white terry-cloth robe—a housewarming gift from my mother—to any meal served before 10:00 A.M., or his drinking Johnnie Walker Black during daytime brunch?

As I crossed the halfway point, I noticed more people started to follow 300 Sandwiches. Friends as far away as New Delhi followed us on Facebook, and left comments. "So I see E's in the doghouse," some would comment after I'd post about a fight we had. Or, "How was that pulled pork sandwich you made the other day? And who knew E didn't like raw tomatoes?"

The idea of making anyone 300 sandwiches was funny. The blog was supposed to be funny. And many people who read the blog found it funny. But some did not.

I found out just how many people were judging us when I went public.

I decided to reveal myself to the world when I hit the halfway point. I felt comfortable enough in the kitchen to have cooked for others and to have mastered enough sandwiches—lamb burgers, Reubens, grilled cheeses, and lettuce wraps—that I felt comfortable having other people re-create what I made for E.

After a year, I had collected enough stories about E and me to be entertaining, and enough recipes to be informative to those equally obsessed with sandwiches. But I also wanted inspiration from other people's recipes and their tales of love and food. I thought it would be fun to share our experience with other like-minded foodie couples. One hundred fifty sandwiches would be a good point to welcome strangers into our wacky kitchen, and to hear other families' stories around cooking.

And what better place to tell that story, our zany story of a girl seeking an engagement ring from her boyfriend by making him sandwiches, than the always entertaining, sometimes polarizing *New York Post*?

The features department of the *Post* is run by Margi Conklin, a whip-smart editor who knew how to package stories for maximum impact. I knew how my story would be published—Page Six reporter and independent gal about town puts on her apron and races home to make sandwiches in order to woo her man. It was a provocative storyline, with great art and photo potential.

"When do you have time to make all these sandwiches between your job and going out at night for Page Six?" Margi asked.

"I don't know. I just don't sleep much these days."

"Are you ready to expose your relationship to the world?" she asked. "Are you ready for what that will bring?"

"Yeah, why not?" What could be worse than the judgment I'd already received from family and friends?

I carefully crafted an essay about the launch of 300 Sandwiches—emphasizing how E cooked me hundreds of meals before he blurted out those fateful words and how I was grateful for said lovingly made meals. I wrote that I made the sandwiches because it was about the journey of growing close to someone, versus actually manipulating him into proposing. I made E sound witty but not too demanding or chauvinistic. I made myself sound open to the challenge, but not desperate for marriage. I made the story sound impossibly saccharine, meticulously crafting our image, the snapshot of our relationship and the journey to make 300 sandwiches in a heartfelt 1,200 words.

I invited the *Post* photographers to come inside our Brooklyn apartment and photograph E and me, together, eating and interacting with each other. It was the first glimpse anyone would see of me cooking. I made a steak banh mi for that day's sandwich, #163, both to post on the blog and for the *New York Post* to photograph, and I had extra groceries in case I had to make more than one. The steak banh mi photographed well, with leafy green cilantro and bright strips of orange carrot layering the seared meat.

The morning the photographers arrived from the *Post*, I cleaned the house, put on the soulful-but-not-too-urban sounds of Mayer Hawthorne, and had a pot of coffee brewing on the counter. E and I had gone to buy muffins at Almondine Bakery down the street, and put them out in an oversize serving bowl on the counter.

For the photo shoot, I wanted to look like a powerful housewife. Sexy, but subtly sexy. Alluring, but still nurturing. In control, but soft. I picked out a red form-fitting dress with a small flower print that showed off my legs and tiny waist, but still covered my cleavage. The makeup artist primped me, applying cherry red lipstick and false eyelashes between questions about the blog. I stood in my kitchen, looking like a modern-day Clair Huxtable. Inside, I was Sheryl Sandberg: every move, every pose, every image planned out in my head, in control of how I projected myself. Leaning in like a pro.

"What should I wear?" E asked.

I manipulated what E looked like as well. I wanted him to look natural. Not like a pig, but also not contrived. "Whatever you want, but look like you. And don't dress up." He settled on his favorite G-Star jeans and a black short-sleeved ribbed shirt.

We posed for photographs as I made a new sandwich and stood with various foods in my hand. E stood so proud, almost in awe of everything that was going on in our kitchen. He then sat with me on the couch, looking at me lovingly as I held sandwiches up to his nose. I fed the photographer and the stylist the steak banh mi and my turkey pear club sandwich—turkey with bacon, lettuce, and pears (a substitute for raw tomatoes, which E will not tolerate). There were no sandwiches left by the time the photo shoot was over.

Two weeks passed, and finally on a Tuesday afternoon, I got word that my story would be in the next day's paper. I saw a glimpse of it on the page and it looked every bit as campy as I expected. "I Wooed My Man with a Sandwich" was the headline. E sat on the couch with a homemade sandwich under his nose while I held the plate, a generous helping of toned leg flashing out underneath the hemline of my red flowered dress. "Genius," I thought. This was going to get attention.

At 8:00 that night, the story went up on the *New York Post* website. The Internet slowly read my words about love and sandwiches, and I watched the traffic numbers slowly creep up as my photo sat on the *NYPost.com* home page.

When I got home, E and I celebrated the story going live with a bottle of champagne and takeout. Of all days to relieve myself of sandwich duty, this was a good one.

Then came the haters.

The Internet trolls who know everything, who smell bullshit from miles away, the pundits, those who know oh-so-much more than everyone else. I knew they'd come.

You know that movie *Night of the Living Dead,* when the otherwise healthy couple had to run from the zombies that fed on the living? The zombies multiplied as they mauled people, infected them, spreading the disease that turned people into crazed predators. One by one, the functioning population turned into the walking dead, climbing over one another to get to the next victims, attacking them like rabid dogs on a tenderloin.

Internet haters operate in similar fashion.

E and I ate breakfast as we fielded calls from family and friends who'd read the story. By the end of the morning E wondered, "How long do you think it will take until the Internet haters hop on the bandwagon?"

"I give it until noon," I said.

Before we left the house, I grabbed E's hand, then looked him in the eye. "Listen, people, online and offline, are going to say things. Mostly mean. But the only people whose opinions matter are those who share blood, and those who write checks. If our employers aren't mad, if our family isn't mad, then everyone else can jump in a lake."

He smiled. "Okay." We headed to work.

When I arrived at the *Post,* our social media team said it had been inundated with tweets, emails, and blog posts about my story. "You're on *Jezebel*," they called out. "You're on *Gawker*." "You're on *Drudge Report*." "You're on *Huffington Post*." "You're on *Time.com*!" *Time* freaking *magazine* had an opinion about my relationship?

The blog posts on 300 Sandwiches ranged from colorful to ignorant:

—"Bitch, Make Me 300 Sandwiches, Orders Beautiful Woman's Boyfriend" *(Gawker)*
—"300 Sandwiches: Bogus Anti Feminist Project or Genius One-way Ticket to Wedded Bliss?" *(Agogo)*
—"Why '300 Sandwiches' Is a Misguided Kind of Romance" *(Huffington Post)*
—"Liberal Feminists Go Insane about Woman Making Sandwiches for Her Boyfriend" (*Right Wing News;* one of the better articles in defense of sandwiches)
—"Il lui promet le mariage, en échange de 300 sandwiches." (*Elle* France)
—"女孩为男友做300个三明治 被男友求婚(双语) (Japanese food blog. No idea what it means.)

~~~~~~

The tweets were even worse. #300feministsandwiches became a rallying cry on Twitter to stand up against my antifemale blog (boy, these people didn't read a damn thing on the site, did they?). People were so angry that "a modern woman was living the punch line of a sexist joke." Someone even launched a spoof blog, Ordering 300 Sandwiches: A Lazy Girl's Guide to Love.

Our parents were in near tears after reading the nasty comments online. "Who the hell do these people think they are!" my mom shouted.

"Mom, don't read the Internet," I told her.

"But how can they write this stuff about you and they don't even know you two? Did they not understand it was supposed to be funny? Did they not see E does most of the cooking?" she defended.

"Nope, they didn't. Welcome to the Internet."

She sighed. And cursed. "I'm going to write these assholes back and tell them what's really going on!"

"Mom, there are too many assholes on the Internet to respond to. You'll be writing until you're dead."

Somehow my take-charge "I'll show you" attitude was misconstrued as a woman getting back in the kitchen after women had fought so long to break out of it and to be seen as equals to men. A throwback for feminism, a desperation for marriage. Most missed the fact that my boyfriend made a joke, and I tried to one-up him. They saw "man demands, woman, make me a sandwich." And they pounced.

The feminists called me desperate, shameless, a detriment to the feminist movement, a publicity whore. The worst example of a woman ever to check the "F" box on an application for a driver's license. I was none of those things. I wasn't crafty enough to do this just for publicity. I am public enough as a reporter on Page Six—my email is in the freaking paper!

If I were that desperate to get married, I would have had 300 damn sandwiches made in a weekend. I would have laid out bread, cheese, meat, and mustard in a row and made them all in an assembly line a la McDonald's—no flavor, no taste, but hundreds served daily—screaming "Remember, I'm a size five ring!" over my shoulder as I stacked each sandwich.

What was my crime? I hadn't taken off my clothes for publicity. I did not pose for the photo shoot in a lacy negligee and high heels. E and I had not made a sex tape and "leaked" it on the Internet like so many of the famous names I had written about in Page Six. I had simply made sandwiches for my boyfriend—in between working ten hours a day at the biggest gossip column in the world—and women were offended. What I saw as a light-hearted way to honor my parents' tradition—and honor my love—others saw as a betrayal.

By the end of the day, the images from the photo shoot—and our Facebook pages, our LinkedIn feeds, and party photos from various events I'd attended—were all over the Internet along with the story.

E texted me:

> The most universally disliked cockroach in all of tech journalism linked to my LinkedIn profile and tried to draw my old client into the fray, like that was really necessary.

I wrote:

> What do they think they're going to find?

Perhaps they could get him fired from his job. Would that be restitution for my having made him a few sandwiches?

I felt exposed, more so than I'd expected. Is this what celebrities and other public figures feel like when I cover them in Page Six? Is this what happens when people interpret a person's marital status, employment history, intelligence, and moral standing from their Facebook and Twitter feeds?

I could actually sympathize with stars like Kim Kardashian and Kanye West, who at the time were engaged to be married, to the delight of no one anywhere. My friends and I had groaned daily about how this overexposed, self-indulgent couple were too despicable for words. We passed all sorts of judgment based on what we saw on television and Twitter. Yet none of us had spent more than two minutes with either of them. (I have actually since then spent two minutes with Kim, and I can say this: She is a nice person. No matter if she is a publicity hound, she always says please and thank you.)

The same was happening to E and me. None of these bloggers knew us. Many knew my work, and my writing, which is why they thankfully called me successful. But no one knew us as a couple.

They had no idea of our dry sense of humor. They didn't know how E had been there for me in my darkest hour when my father was diagnosed with cancer, and how that was why he really deserved my love—and that was the real reason why I chose to make the man 300 sandwiches.

I could take the criticism of myself. I got us into this mess. I launched the site. So I could shine off my proverbial armor, whatever venom was spewed our way from haters. But the haters went after E in a more spiteful manner. They insulted his looks. They had this image of him as this chauvinistic, potbellied sloth sitting on the couch ordering me to make him a damn sandwich. Some amazingly suggested he was too lazy to make his own sandwiches. Some even likened him to a slave master keeping me as his house Negro. Oh, yeah, they went there.

From the most bigoted commenters—most of these, sadly, from other African American readers—I got a number of dreadful posts that considered me a shame to my own race because I was cooking for my white boyfriend. I could not believe that in 2014, a day where interracial couples are shown on television without fanfare, and an era where the president of the United States is a black man, anyone would throw Mammy references toward me, an African American woman writing a blog about cooking for my white boyfriend as we headed toward engagement.

No one was clear on what my crime was—was it the cooking thing, or was it the dating a white man thing? Or was it cooking for the white man I'm dating? And what should I have done when E told me I was 300 sandwiches away from an engagement ring? Smacked him upside the head with a frying pan? Snapped my fingers in his face, shook my head, and screamed, "Oh, no you didn't?!" Would *that* have made black women look better? That would have played right into the angry black woman stereotype. That, in fact, would have been setting us back a few years, my brothas and sistahs.

All I did was make a few sandwiches because my man, who had cooked just about every meal we shared at home during our relationship, said he liked them. There were far worse things I could have done for love.

Women, black, white, or otherwise, have sacrificed much more for a man's attention. They've stalked men. They've lied to family and friends. They've worn little or no clothing and strutted around bars and nightclubs. They've dated, or worse, married, men solely for money. They've gotten boob jobs or nose jobs or lost weight or otherwise changed their appearances or moral compasses to adjust to the whims of a man. A sandwich for a man who wanted to eat your sandwiches, and then propose marriage, seemed like a downright fair trade in comparison.

E had been more loyal to me than any man, black or white, had been before. He introduced me to his parents and took me home for Christmas the first opportunity he could. Many of my ex-boyfriends, African American or otherwise, couldn't even bother to make me coffee, much less dinner.

But for the record, if E were black and had been as faithful and doting and had asked for 300 sandwiches, he too would have received them as a token of my commitment to him as happy as he made me.

The blogosphere was angry at E for "making me earn my ring," or the perception of him making me earn my ring. And in what could be considered the best display of Internet irony, the haters—gasp!—declared E the Internet's Worst Boyfriend.

"That's quite the accomplishment to become the Internet's Worst Anything. I'll take it!" E said. "I'll start a line of cooking utensils, bath products, and linens!"

Though I was laughing at the haters' shortsightedness, I was amazed that after all that care I took in creating the perfect image of us in that *New York Post* article, our home, our relationship, E as a man, after all of the editing to say the right thing, to look perfect in the photos, to tell the perfect story of our love, most people only read the headline.

And then, Matt Lauer called.

. . .

Okay, somebody who works with Matt Lauer called.

A producer from the *Today* show wanted me to come on the show the next morning and make ten sandwiches on live television. Apparently Matt had seen the site during his morning commute. Well, someone on the show had seen it, anyway.

I had never cooked on live television. I was barely confident enough to cook in front of E. But when you get a call to come on the *Today* show and make food, you transform into Martha Stewart faster than you can say béchamel.

Putting fear of failure aside, I crawled out of myself and watched the shell of my body agree to do the segment, and hand over my recipes and image to the food producers at *Today*. I got into a mindset where I didn't think it was actually me going on television, but a character. I faked it. I didn't fake my love for E, I just faked my confidence.

That night, I planned out my menu and prepped as many vegetables in advance as I could for the sandwiches. I laid out my outfit and packed my purse for the next day with extra makeup and an extra shirt in case I spilled olive oil on what I planned to wear on air.

E picked an oddly conservative outfit: a vest, trousers, and a white button down. He looked like he was going to a wedding. My heart raced. My mouth hung agape. Oh. Please. God. No.

"Are you . . . planning to propose tomorrow?" I asked.

He shrieked, "NO!"

"Oh." *Phew!* But still, he looked dressed for a special occasion. "Then change! You look like you're going to propose."

"Oh, God, then I'll change."

"Yes!" I said. "Don't propose!"

"I'm not proposing!"

"Good! I don't want you to propose! Yet! Like, on air! You know what I mean."

That would have been the worst idea ever. I wasn't ready.

Wow, that was a reality check. After two and a half years of dating, eighteen months of living together, and 174 sandwiches, it dawned on me that perhaps I was not yet ready to be married.

What would happen if he did propose tomorrow? On the *Today* show, no less? Would I have said no? Would I have grinned and mumbled, "Okay, sure," but then have been unsure? I thought I had this all figured out. I thought I wanted to get married and have babies. That was the plan!

Maybe my heart had not caught up to my brain.

And there we were, in front of my sandwiches, in the *Today* show's studios, millions of Americans watching, when Matt goes for the jugular: "When she hits number three hundred, will you get down on one knee and will you propose?"

I expected E to play coy. "Of course," E replied.

"Yes?" Matt asked.

"Of course."

Of course. Really?

"Hasn't she proved her love to you already?" Savannah Guthrie asked.

E stood up an inch taller, and threw his hand in front of him. "I would have married her without one sandwich."

BOOM.

Savannah turned to me. "I guess you wish you would have known that before you started making all of these sandwiches, huh?"

Sort of, I thought. "I would have saved a ton of money on groceries."

sandwich

#159

SUBSTITUTE FOR TOMATOES—
TURKEY AND PEAR CLUB SANDWICH

I made this for the day of our New York Post *photo shoot. E doesn't like raw tomatoes, so I usually roast tomatoes when I use them on sandwiches. Or, in the summer, I substitute peaches or apples. On this BLT, I used pear, which pairs (ha!) well with crispy bacon and crunchy romaine lettuce.*

3 slices bacon
3 slices whole wheat bread
2 tablespoons red currant jam
4 to 6 romaine lettuce leaves
½ pear, sliced
4 to 5 slices turkey

Fry the bacon to desired crispness. Toast the bread. Slather one side of all the slices of bread with red currant jam. On the bottom pieces of bread, layer some of the lettuce, some pear slices, and some turkey. Add another slice of bread, lettuce, turkey, bacon, then finish with the last piece of bread. Slice in half. Makes 1 sandwich.

STEPHANIE SMITH

sandwich

#178

PEOPLE ARE TALKING—
GRILLED CHEESE AND PEAR SANDWICH

This sandwich came from a woman named Mary Beth in Walnut Creek, California, who touched me when she sent me the recipe after our Today show segment. She thought fondly of her ex-husband because he'd made her this sandwich. "Here's a recipe you can try ... it was one that my ex-husband (we are still friends) would make on weekend mornings prior to our marriage ending." I had to try it.

2 tablespoons unsalted butter
2 slices olive bread
2 teaspoons honey mustard
3 or 4 slices Manchego or Comté cheese (or any mild cheese)
1 pear, sliced
salt and pepper

Butter the bread on one side, then flip over. Spread mustard on the bare sides, then layer on cheese and pear. Sprinkle with salt and pepper, then finish with bread. Toast the sandwich in a panini press for about 5 minutes, long enough for the cheese to melt. (Or use stovetop instructions on page 55.) Cut in half. Makes 1 sandwich.

SEVENTEEN

Women online may not have been admiring me. But part of the 300 sandwiches concept was inspired by women I admired, women who cooked. For example, I met E's grandmother Sharon, Renee's mother, during my first Christmas with E. She and I bonded on the couch in the living room, sipping white wine on Christmas Day after brunch. Sharon had signs of dementia, but given this was our first meeting, she went through the archives of her mind to tell me everything about her family: all of her children, their families, their kids, the ones who had even passed away too soon. She knew all of the rough details. E filled in the rest.

Grandmother Adams, E told me, was a mix between Julia Child and Escoffier. She cooked Thanksgiving dinner for thirty each year, on her own. (I could barely handle dinner for twelve without help.) She was happily married to E's grandfather, Dr. Vincent Adams, from the time she was nineteen until his death in 2005. Sharon was so loyal to him, E told me, she cooked his favorite meal faithfully for years.

"Spam," he told me. "Of course, Sharon made him better quality meals in a snap. But on occasion, with a wink and a smile, because he loved it, she would make him a plate of good ol', straight out of the can Spam."

Sharon, as E recalled, was an old-fashioned kind of gal. As in, E always addressed her as Grandma, not Nana or Grammy or anything cutesy. (I always called my grandmothers "Granny.") Sharon was raised in Grosse Pointe, at a time when the only people of dark skin were likely to be the maids or butlers of the people with last names like Ford, Dodge, or Alger. She dressed for dinner, always in pearls or pressed slacks or polished shoes, and, in her affinity for fur coats, could be outdone only by her own mother.

Grandma Adams grew up at a time when Detroit was a booming automotive town, and then a thriving Motown scene, then dissipated into a less desirable city. Now, just miles from her old colonial style home off of Lake Shore Drive, Detroit was falling apart. And now her grandson was about to marry a black woman. How times had changed.

The next Christmas, her memory was failing. She barely remembered me when I walked into Renee's home and handed her a gift of a sweet-smelling candle. But she doubled back to me later, presenting me with a gift, and said, "Yes, we had wine last Christmas, how are you? Are you and Eric married yet?"

The following summer, two weeks after E's family was all together for a family wedding, she passed away. E flew home for the service. He returned with his grandmother's china. "One thing to cross off the registry. Future wedding invitees can contribute to our World Tour Fund instead," E said.

I didn't know that wasn't the only trinket he'd gotten from one of his grandmothers.

We were hosting Thanksgiving once again. E's mom couldn't make it out this time, but we invited fifteen of our friends anyway, now that we were practiced at hosting the holidays. We started our prep on Tuesday night, racing to the grocery store to pick up our turkey and other vegetables. That night, after work, a big Nor'easter bringing sleet and rain and winds howled across the tristate area. We fought the elements, driving our car to Fairway, about three miles south of our place, to pick up food. The storm brought respite from the hordes of T-day shoppers, at least. We trekked home damp, with all of our goods, including wine.

E helped me get the groceries into our lobby before parking the car nearly two blocks away. I unloaded all of the soggy bags into our apartment, and started organizing the food. I couldn't wait to crack open that bottle of pinot noir we'd bought.

A few minutes later, E banged through the door, wetter than I was, his umbrella dripping droplets onto our hardwood floor. We stared at each other. "We have some work ahead of us."

He disappeared into the office to take off his shoes and wipe his face while I unloaded the groceries. He returned, and stood near the end of the counter. The enormity of yet another holiday of us together hit me. Despite the cooking ahead, the cleaning the house, the hosting of friends, I turned to E and declared, "There's no one else I'd rather spend Thanksgiving with."

E walked across the kitchen and hugged me. "I have a present for you."

I expected a corkscrew so we could crack open that wine.

Instead he turned and pulled out a pouch from the music box on the table. That was too small to be a corkscrew. What the . . .

He held the small velvet pouch nervously in his hand. Then, he walked slowly, nervously toward me.

OH GOOOD LORDON'TLETTHISBEANENGAGEMENT RINGOHMYGODDON'TLETTHISBE . . . holy hell is he going to propose in the kitchen . . . like this?

"This is not an engagement ring," he said. "This is a promise."

I stopped breathing as he flipped over the small pouch. Out popped the daintiest ring. Maybe a half carat, with three smaller diamonds on each side set in white gold. It was vintage.

"This was my grandmother's ring," E said.

Sharon.

"My grandfather gave it to her while he was a poor med student, straight out of World War II. She was nineteen when she got engaged," E said. "She wanted you to have it."

Shouldn't his mom have it? I was just a girlfriend. We weren't even close to being engaged when E's grandmother passed away. I must have made quite the impression over that glass of wine at Christmas two years ago.

"My mother sent it to me to give to you. Both of us feel that Grandma would have wanted you to wear it."

I said nothing. I just stared motionless for a minute. I couldn't believe someone thought highly enough of me to give me their family heirloom. The flashes of past relationships flew before me—the guys who didn't think highly enough of me to call me back after two dates, the one who didn't think highly enough of me to stay faithful, the one who didn't think enough to remember my birthday, the one who didn't think enough to introduce me to his parents. None of them thought I was good enough.

Until now.

A woman who knew that I would be part of the next generation of the family, but also knew she might not live long enough to witness it, wanted me to know she thought highly enough of me to welcome me to her family.

I was honored.

Surprisingly, fear also shot through my body. I was scared. Scared that this was it. Scared that this was sort of replacing my engagement and there would be no surprise afterward. Scared that this was now the real deal, and we were no longer playing house and we had to really think of ourselves as a couple.

Scared that the ring wouldn't fit.

Sharon had been a small lady.

E grabbed my right ring finger. "It's small, so you might have to get it sized."

And then he put the ring on my finger. It fit perfectly.

"So what do you think about that?"

I looked and stared. I knew it must have taken him so much courage to give me that ring. So much. And I just kept staring. For something that was so small, the weight of its meaning was pretty heavy. I felt like I was engaged.

Fear left my body, and instead of being scared of not measuring up, I was inspired to love E even more than I had in our two years together.

After a full minute of silence, I finally got my thoughts together.

"Honey, I know what it must have taken for your mother to want me to have this. I mean, your mom and her mom were so close. I just . . ."

"Well, let's call her right now," E suggested.

We rang his mom on her cell phone, but she didn't pick up. She called back a minute later.

"Did we wake you?"

"I was up getting some water. What's up?"

"She loves the ring," E said.

I took the phone, and blabbered on about being honored and loved and touched and thankful and I think it all came out in English, but to this day I'm not sure if it did.

"Oh, honey, you're welcome," she said. "Sharon was very fond of you, she loved you and wanted you and Eric to be happy. She would have wanted you to have it."

Apparently Sharon had been asking for months when E and I were finally going to get engaged. She knew nothing of the blog or 300 sandwiches. "Mom always asked, 'Well, when is it? Soon? Soon?' And I'd say, 'Yes, Mom.' And she'd say, 'Well, let's get this show on the road, then!' I'm sure she's looking down and happy that you're happy."

I thought about my father. Was he thinking the same thing? He had never put pressure on us to hurry up and finish. When he was at another round of chemo, did he think he would be watching this from above, as opposed to walking me down the aisle?

I wanted him to be with me.

I hoped I could get these sandwiches done in enough time.

Until then, for tonight, I enjoyed the ring that was given to me, which meant more than anything Harry Winston or Tiffany could create.

GRILLED CHEESES
FOR WHEN YOU'RE FEELING CHEESY

There are as many combinations for grilled cheese as there are cheeses in the world. I made more than fifteen versions before I got engaged. Here are the standouts.

STEPHANIE SMITH

CRANBERRY AND BRIE GRILLED CHEESE

Brie is on my Forbidden Foods list. I know—I'm weird about creamy cheeses. But this grilled cheese sandwich is pretty great. I made this one on a snowy day right after Christmas, with leftover cranberry sauce and cheese from a holiday spread we'd set out for company.

**1 to 2 tablespoons unsalted butter
4 slices bread
2 tablespoons mustard
6 to 8 slices of Brie (or enough generous chunks
to melt down ooey gooey)
2 tablespoons cranberry sauce**

Smear butter on one side of bread. Flip the bread over and smear mustard on the other side. On the bottom pieces of bread, lay slices of Brie, then drizzle cranberry sauce on top. Finish with another slice of bread, mustard side down, and place in a nonstick pan on medium heat. (Or use a panini press.) Grill 2 to 3 minutes each side, flipping once. Cut in half to serve. Makes 2 sandwiches.

BRIE AND PEAR GRILLED CHEESE

To help with tax woes: April 15 isn't fun for anyone—even if you're getting a refund, you're still annoyed by the paperwork.

2 tablespoons unsalted butter
4 slices bread
2 tablespoons strawberry-balsamic jam
(any strawberry jam will do)
2 tablespoons Brie, softened
½ pear, sliced

Spread butter on one side of each piece of bread, strawberry jam on the other sides. With the buttered sides down on your work surface, smear Brie on bottom slices. Stack the slices of pear, and finish with the other pieces of bread, jam side down. Toast the sandwich in a panini press or nonstick pan with a sandwich press on top. Brown until the cheese is melted, about 5 minutes. Makes 2 sandwiches.

sandwich

#108

GOAT CHEESE AND BASIL GRILLED CHEESE

You can find both fig butter and truffle butter at a gourmet grocery. Grill this when you're in a gourmet type of mood.

1 teaspoon truffle butter
2 slices bread
2 tablespoons fig butter
4 to 5 leaves fresh basil
4 to 5 slices Drunken Goat Cheese

Spread truffle butter sparingly on one side of the bread. Spread fig butter on the other side. Lay basil leaves on top of the fig butter, then slices of cheese. Finish with the other piece of bread, fig butter side down. Toast in a panini press or on the stovetop for about 3 minutes, until cheese is melted. Slice in half to serve. Makes 1 sandwich.

sandwich

#204

GOAT CHEESE, WALNUT, AND HONEY GRILLED CHEESE

It's late, and you've got the munchies. This goat cheese, honey, and chopped walnut sandwich, warmed, is great for those night-owl cravings.

1 tablespoon unsalted butter
2 slices bread
2 tablespoons goat cheese
¼ cup chopped walnuts
1 tablespoon honey

Melt the butter in a nonstick pan over medium heat. Smear the bottom piece of bread with goat cheese. Sprinkle with chopped walnuts and drizzle with honey. Finish with the other piece of bread. Warm in the pan for about 3 minutes, flipping once. Remove, slice, and serve. Makes 1 sandwich.

STEPHANIE SMITH

sandwich

#224

MOZZARELLA AND ROASTED TOMATO GRILLED CHEESE

An easy Italian grilled cheese with mozzarella and roasted tomatoes, the only way E would accept tomatoes on a sandwich.

4 small tomatoes, quartered
2 tablespoons chopped fresh parsley
3 tablespoons olive oil
1 garlic clove, crushed
salt and pepper
handful of arugula leaves (about ⅓ cup)
4 slices bread
4 or 5 slices mozzarella cheese
1 tablespoon unsalted butter

Roast the tomatoes: Preheat the oven to 400 degrees. In a shallow oven-safe dish, place the quartered tomatoes, parsley, 2 tablespoons of the olive oil, garlic, salt, and pepper. Stir lightly to coat the tomatoes, pop in the oven, and roast for about ½ hour.

In a small bowl, lightly toss the arugula with the remaining tablespoon of olive oil. On the bottom pieces of bread, stack cheese, tomato, and arugula. Finish with the other pieces of bread.

Toast in a panini press, or melt a tablespoon of butter on medium heat in a nonstick pan and warm the sandwich for about 3 minutes. Remove, slice, and serve. Makes 2 sandwiches.

PART THREE

"Hurry Up with Those Sandwiches"

EIGHTEEN

Sandwich #199 was when I became a real woman: I roasted my first chicken.

Roast chicken. It's instant Sunday dinner. It's a "come home from church and get yourself a plate" meal. It's dinner-party fabulous. It's wifey material.

It's also the first thing I could say with confidence that I mastered better than E.

Serious foodies claim you can judge a cook by her roast chicken. It's a simple process with simple ingredients that can come out either wonderfully succulent and flavorful or bland and dry.

Julia Child has a recipe. Ina Garten has one. *Glamour* magazine has one that claims it's so good, a man will propose to you after you make it. E's mom, Renee, has one too. In essence it's all the same—chicken, kosher salt, pepper, lemon, butter, and herbs of your choosing. Roast in the oven for about an hour or until brown. The difference in all of these recipes is what you do with the chicken, or yourself, while it's roasting. Baste or not baste. Cook under high heat and reduce it gradually or keep at a steady higher temperature for a shorter time. Pour generous glass of wine, sit on couch, watch *Will & Grace* reruns, remove chicken from oven when glass of wine is empty.

Whenever E and I finish up a large project—for example, covering a week's worth of fashion shows and late-night parties during Fashion Week for the *Post,* or writing a month's worth of code for a new app—we make a tradition of having a victory dinner at Blue Ribbon Brasserie in Soho. Blue Ribbon was founded by a group of guys from New Jersey, and the menu is full of good, fresh food with a large focus on the raw bar. It's downtown New York's soul food. The lighting is perfect, not too dark and not too bright, their playlists of '70s and '80s soul tunes is played at a pleasant decibel level. The dining room seats about seventy-five—big enough not to be a hole in the wall, but small enough to still feel intimate—and more important, it's open till 4:00 A.M. nightly.

We usually meet at Blue Ribbon on Friday night at the end of our long week. The wait for a table is usually long, as they don't take reservations, but pleasant, because the patrons you're keeping company with at the bar while you wait are there on a date, or with their long-time domestic partners for a casual nightcap, or have arrived from out of town and are just excited to breathe the same air as the downtown locals. Somehow, the bespectacled manager who presides over the dining room finds a table for us before E and I can finish our first round of drinks.

We always devour two things at the restaurant. One, their warm house bread, perfectly spongy on the inside with a crisp, browned crust; they make it in-house and it always arrives at the table still steaming. Doesn't matter if you're trying to avoid gluten or you're on Atkins, you will eat the bread. And you will love it.

The second thing is their roast chicken, which comes in a few large breast slices with the skin still on and accompanied by sweet potatoes and collard greens. The chicken is succulent: moist but not too greasy, with the perfect amount of lemon zest. Though I am one of those weird food segregationists—I do not permit my food items to touch one another on the plate, so that the flavors from one food do not blend or overpower another—I do like to cut a small piece of chicken, then stack a small amount of greens and sweet potato on my fork, and eat all three together. It tastes like a holiday, a special occasion. "You somehow made it through yet another Fashion Week, love," E would say as I swallowed my dinner and smiled.

E's mom taught him to roast a chicken during one of her at-home cooking lessons. When E was in grade school, Renee described roasting chicken as if Foghorn Leghorn sat in the oven, getting a tan.

"I once taught him how to roast chicken by giving the chicken personality and voice," she said. As she slowly applied butter or oil to the bird, she pretended to be the voice of the chicken, saying, "Ah, a little to the left, that's nice. Ooh, little to the right, that's nice too."

As the bird cooked, it "talked back" to E. While in the oven, the chicken would call out, "It's getting a little warm in here." Or, "Okay, it's getting kind of hot in here" or "Wow, I'm getting tan," Renee told me.

E was so enthralled with the chicken that he wrote a story about the talkative, sun-loving bird for the children's magazine *Highlights,* which young kids between the ages of four and eight read like adults read *People* magazine. E won first place in a writing competition for the magazine, calling his essay "Silly Chicken."

"Unfortunately they changed the name to 'Funny Chicken,' and edited and changed much of what he had written for publication," Renee said. "They sent him a recipe book as an award."

I was in the middle of a good *Will & Grace* marathon on one particular Saturday afternoon and did not feel like standing in front of the hot stove for hours making dinner. E was in the office, cranking away on some code for some app that allowed users to accomplish some mundane chore right through their smartphones without talking to people or taking out their wallet (which, it seems, is what most good apps do).

We were in for the night because the weather outside was dreadful—a blustery November night, right before Thanksgiving. I had bought a four-pound whole chicken from the grocery store earlier that day, and gathered my ingredients. I read a few recipes before I got started, and every one of them recommended you rub salt all over the bird and refrigerate for a few hours to let the salt moisten the skin. Then, let the bird come to room temperature, rub your butter and spices all over, and pop it in the oven.

I could handle that.

A few hours before I was going to fire up the oven, E popped his head out of the office to help. "I was looking at a few recipes. Some suggest you salt the bird for a few hours before you start cooking."

"I know," I said. "I just rubbed the entire chicken in salt and pepper. When this episode is over, then I'll pop the bird in the oven."

"Well, look at you," he said, smiling.

At sandwich #12, I would have had E babysit me through the process. Or he would have made the entire dinner while I savored a glass of wine and flipped through his Spotify playlist. But now, after some practice in the kitchen, I had this.

I stuffed some thyme and lemon inside the bird, trussed it with twine, and popped it in the oven on 400 degrees. And then I sat on the couch, only getting up to baste the bird every thirty minutes and to refill my glass of wine until the meat was ready.

The browned, roasted chicken looked so beautiful on the roasting rack, the carrots and onions sitting snugly around the meat. E was satisfied with dinner, like, really satisfied. "Honey, I'm impressed," E told me.

We ate the chicken with a quick arugula, pear, and Parmesan salad, and I was convinced this could become a Sunday-night staple.

THE 300 SANDWICHES QUICK AND DIRTY
RECIPE FOR ROAST CHICKEN

Everyone has a different school of thought on roast chicken. My school is the University of He Liked It So It Must Be Good. E, he of the discerning palate, thought my roast chicken was divine. I would do this anytime guests call at 2:00 P.M. to say they're coming over at 6:00. Get bird, season well, and cook. Play cards or dominoes while bird roasts. Let bird rest, then serve with veggies of your choice for dinner. The next day, make roast chicken sandwiches.

1 4-to-5-pound whole chicken
salt and pepper
4 to 5 slices lemon
4 to 5 sprigs thyme
4 to 5 sprigs rosemary
¼ cup (½ stick) unsalted butter, softened

Lightly sprinkle salt over the entire bird and place it in the refrigerator for an hour or two. (Some people do this overnight. I don't have that kind of forethought, so I simply let it sit for a few hours.) Then remove it from the refrigerator and bring the bird to room temperature before cooking.

Preheat the oven to 425 degrees. Wash the bird with warm water, and pat dry with a paper towel. Season the bird with salt and pepper. Stuff the cavity with lemon slices, thyme, and rosemary. Slather the skin of the bird with half the butter. Tie the legs together with twine, tuck the wings under the body cavity, and pop in the oven. Roast at 425 degrees for 20 minutes. Baste with more butter, and turn the heat down to 350 degrees. Cook for 1 hour, checking and basting bird with the remaining butter after 30 minutes. Remove from the oven, let rest, carve, and serve.

SATURDAY NIGHTS IN YOUR THIRTIES—
CHICKEN AND WAFFLE BLT

Your chicken will be so good, you may not have leftovers. If you do, make these sandwiches the next day for brunch.

**4 Belgian waffles
2 tablespoons Dijon mustard
4 or 5 red leaf lettuce leaves
2 to 3 slices tomato*
4 or 5 slices roast chicken
4 slices bacon**

Toast the waffles. Spread Dijon mustard on the 2 bottom waffles, then stack lettuce, tomatoes, chicken, bacon, and finish with the other 2 waffles. Cut in half on the diagonal. Makes 2 sandwiches.

    * For E's sandwich, I omitted tomatoes. But I refused to for my own.

sandwich
#230

CANDIED BACON
AND HONEY DIJON CHICKEN WRAPS

I originally made this recipe with chicken breasts marinated with honey and mustard and quickly baked in the oven. But this is another good way to use leftover roast chicken—layer it with candied bacon, greens, and mustard on a flatbread. Tasty wraps for lunch or a picnic.

½ cup maple syrup
1 teaspoon smoked paprika
½ tablespoon cinnamon
pinch of chili powder
5 or 6 slices bacon
2 flatbreads
1 tablespoon honey Dijon mustard
4 leaves romaine lettuce
4 to 5 slices leftover roast chicken

Make the candied bacon: Preheat the oven to 350 degrees. In a small bowl, whisk together the syrup and spices. Lay the bacon strips flat on a baking sheet. Spoon the syrup mixture over each side of each bacon slice. (You can use the spoon-and-smooth method, where you spoon some syrup on the bacon, then smooth it over the surface with the back of the spoon. Or, if you like to play with your food, dip the bacon in the syrup, then put the strip between two fingers and run them down the length of each slice. That evenly distributes the syrup and ensures you don't use too much of it.) Pop the baking sheet in the preheated oven for 10 minutes, rotate the pan, and cook for another 10 minutes. Let cool on a wire rack.

Chop the candied bacon. Lay out the flatbreads. Spread a thin layer of honey Dijon mustard on one side of both pieces of bread. Stack each flatbread with lettuce, then chicken, then candied bacon. Wrap up the flatbreads and cut in half to serve. Makes 2 sandwiches.

NINETEEN

Now that I had invited the entire Internet-connected world into our relationship, everyone had an opinion. People judged E, often incorrectly, based on everything I posted on 300sandwiches.com.

Readers deemed E despicable if, for example, he picked off the olives from a sandwich I made him. Whenever we bickered about the dishes or me not having enough time to cook when I came home from my demanding full-time job, people wrote in saying E was too hard on me. "He's too picky!" "He complains too much!" Of course, they would ignore when I wrote he cooked four of the previous dinners for me without complaint.

People were even more opinionated about the engagement.

At sandwich #200, the *Post* asked me to write another story about being 100 sandwiches away from an engagement. But I thought it would be better to hear from E what it was like to be 100 sandwiches away from buying an engagement ring.

E didn't initially respond to the online haters to defend his character, but in a 700-word post, he told America how he really felt about the pressure to propose:

I already know that in the eyes of the public, the stone will never be flawless enough, the ring never shiny enough, and the proposal never perfect enough to satisfy the impeccable taste and boundless prowess of Internet commenters.

And after 300 tasty, lovingly made, and beautifully documented sandwiches—a Herculean yet unnecessary gesture—how could I pos-

sibly measure up? How could my proposal be thoughtful, original, memorable, and beautiful enough to equal or surpass the scale of effort she's given me?

Then, he solicited ideas for how he should propose:

My original ideas—sunrise over Haleakala, fireflies trained to spell out "Marry Me" like in The Nutty Professor II, *full-page ad in the* Post— *now seemed comparatively quaint. Oh, the pressure!*

Facing such lofty expectations, The Internet's Worst Boyfriend® is determined to succeed and impress no matter what, despite a few recent setbacks: My original plan to propose sixty-eight miles above the Earth aboard a Virgin Galactic flight was dashed after the first flights got delayed and I ended up a few hundred grand short of the fare. My backup plan—orchestra, ballpark, cameras rolling—was recently stolen outright by Kanye West. What's the plan now?

A 300-dancer Bollywood proposal spectacular?

300 John Cusacks with boomboxes overhead?

A 300-member flash-mob gospel choir?

A combination of the three? I'm stumped.

Hundreds of people sent emails, comments on 300sandwiches .com and our Facebook page, tweets, and direct messages with proposal ideas:

Do it with a sandwich!

Put the ring in a sandwich!

Go to the Post *and ask them to put an item in Page Six!*

Do it at Yankee Stadium!

One suggestion made me want to run for the hills: "*You should do your engagement on live television.*"

My worst nightmare.

Though I'd put our relationship on public display, I wanted the engagement to stay between us. I didn't need the Kardashians' camera crew covering our engagement. I didn't want any jewelry makers or banquet halls or all-inclusive resorts sponsoring "the engagement event of the year." This was not the Super Bowl. It was not a sport to be observed with hot dogs and a twelve-pack of beer. E's proposal was supposed to be simple and heartfelt. Not scripted.

The engagement was the one event I didn't want control of.

One reader, Peter S., described my feelings to a T:

Eric,

Make the proposal yours and Stephanie's alone. No razzle dazzle, no circus clowns . . . no trying to outdo Kanye.

Finally, someone who understood me. He had a suggestion of his own:

Make it a romantic evening somewhere, perhaps Atlantic City. Spend some time gambling . . . then find a nice deli in some casino. Tell Stephanie, "I want to compare a professional sandwich to yours." Order the sandwich, and as soon as it arrives . . . drop to your knees and propose.

I'll take the romantic evening. But I'll pass on the ring in a sandwich in a casino deli.

sandwich

#205

NAME-CALLING—GREEK SALAD WRAPS

This is an easy, veggie-packed wrap that's great to snack on while you ignore the negative nastiness of others. This wrap is a reminder that a great sandwich is the best revenge.

½ cup diced red bell pepper
½ cup diced green bell pepper
½ cup diced cucumber
1 cup grape or small vine tomatoes, cut into quarters
¼ cup diced radish
¼ cup diced red onion
½ cup crumbled feta cheese
2 tablespoons olive oil
1 tablespoon red wine vinegar
1 teaspoon lemon juice
¼ to ⅓ cup chopped fresh parsley
½ teaspoon herbes de Provence
salt and pepper
2 flatbreads or whole wheat wraps

In a bowl, toss together all the veggies and cheese. Drizzle on the olive oil, vinegar, and lemon juice and coat the veggies thoroughly. Add the herbs and season with salt and pepper to taste. Lay out the flatbreads and scoop the salad down the middle. Fold the bread in, top and bottom, then the sides. Flip over and slice to serve. Makes 2 sandwiches.

TWENTY

Literally speaking, making these 300 sandwiches was all about the pursuit of an engagement ring. But in thirty-some years, I'd never nailed down what I wanted that ring to be.

I had never been to the second floor of Tiffany's, where they have the engagement rings on display (so I've been told). Nor to Harry Winston or Cartier. I looked at engagement rings in photos or in magazines only to report for Page Six on who received or bought one whenever some celebrity or socialite got engaged to some banker, lawyer, or rapper—or had to sell back said ring when the relationship ended in tears.

I had not thought about my own engagement ring until, at sandwich #200, E asked me what I wanted.

"Um . . ." I said. All I knew is that I preferred a square shape to a round stone. "Square cut?"

"Square cut? Huh. Do you want a princess cut? Emerald? Royal Asscher? Radiant?"

"Aren't they the same?" I asked.

"No, they're not," E said.

"Well, um, er . . ." I felt the pressure to say *something*.

"Okay, what type of setting?"

"Um, square setting?"

"Oh, boy." He shook his head.

Somewhere between sandwich #150 and now, E had been doing his research. He knew what D versus J color rating meant. He knew what an SI1 versus a VS2 was. I knew nothing. In fact, I confused "karat" and "carat" with E because I didn't think that hard about my own diamond (I quickly googled the difference: Karat is a measure of gold purity; carat measures diamond or precious stone weight).

He had contacted diamond miners, rough-diamond geologists, NGO activists, professors, journalists, and authors who have written about diamonds, as well as diamond wholesalers to learn about the manufacturing processes. E shopped vigorously for loose stones on various websites. He approached diamond buying as he did building an app—he looked up every single journal, guidebook, manual, article, footnote, and text message written on the topic to thoroughly understand the subject matter before talking about it.

"Well, I guess I have no clue as to what I want," I said.

E smiled, wiping his hands with a dish towel. "If I show you something, you have to promise not to freak out," he said.

"I promise."

He walked toward our office in the rear of our apartment, disappearing around the corner. Wasn't the whole idea of making the 300 sandwiches to get an engagement ring? Maybe I'd forgotten all that while I was trying to perfect my roast chicken.

E walked back toward me quickly with his iPad in hand. "I've been looking at a few things," he said. He pulled up the browser on his iPad, bookmarked with rings he'd picked out. One of them was a sculptural onyx ring by David Yurman. It didn't look like your typical engagement ring, but it was a statement piece, something that stood out in a crowd.

Another was a yellow diamond ring, another oversize stone, but one that didn't look too engagement-y.

I smiled and looked at him, thinking that his selection of these types of rings must reflect what he thought of me as a person—a standout, a piece of art, unique. But I would have no idea what engagement ring I really liked until I saw one on my finger.

"I think we should go to a store and try some of these on," I said.

"We have no idea how they look in person, on a real hand. Just to look. No pressure to buy. Just research. Would that be okay?"

He looked at me. "For research. I think that would be smart."

I knew my mother was going to insert herself into the ring-buying process. She covets two things: jewelry and handbags. My mom wore rings and bracelets every day—even with sweatpants—and preferred jewelry as gifts for her birthday or for Christmas. She couldn't walk past a jewelry store without browsing or chatting up the sales clerks, even if only to swap notes about the latest designs. I told my mother about my conversation about diamonds with E.

"You did what?" my mom asked.

"We talked about engagement rings."

"Has he proposed yet?"

"No, but he asked me what I liked."

"Huh," Mom said, impressed. "Well, what *do* you like?"

"I have no idea."

"Lord," she said, "how are you my child?"

"He has some idea of what *he* likes."

"Does he now?!" she said, her voice rising an octave.

"I'll email you some photos."

I sent her the photos of the two rings that E picked out while we were on the phone. "Let's see here." She inspected the photos one by one, making low humming noises to herself that sounded like an anteater examining lunch.

"What's this first one here, the black one? That's an engagement ring?"

"Well, that's what he thought I'd like. He particularly liked the setting."

She mumbled. "Mmm yeah, but it's not really an engagement ring."

"Well, I didn't want anything too traditional."

"But that looks more like a cocktail ring," she said.

"Okayeee," I said defensively. "What about the other one?"

She took a moment to look at the second one, which was smaller. "Mmm, I mean, they're good as cocktail rings, but not your engagement ring."

I had envisioned Mom and me giddily browsing through the Tiffany and Harry Winston websites and cooing over settings and diamonds we liked, even if they were wildly outside E's price range. I thought my mother would be open to whatever I would like for a ring. But I was surprised she would be just as judgmental as the Internet about the engagement ring. Perhaps I didn't want a traditional engagement ring, some cookie-cutter diamond that looked like it was ordered from Diamonds R Us during an insomnia-driven shopping spree. Did Mom want me to have a gaudy five-carat marquise-cut diamond on a gold band, like something one of those Mafia wives in *Goodfellas* would wear?

"You're saying my boyfriend has bad taste," I snipped.

"I'm not saying that!"

"That's what it sounds like!" I defended him.

"No, what I'm saying is you have to think about wearing this every day, and with a wedding band. You might want to consider something more classic. Also, the entire world is going to be looking at this ring, so you need to pick something that people will perceive as an engagement ring."

Not only did I have to make sandwiches my blog followers would like, I had to pick my ring based on what readers in Uzbekistan would like, too?

"Why can't I just enjoy the whole ring-shopping process?" I said. "Why do I have to fit myself into a box?"

"Don't be snippy, Stef!" Mom said.

"You said my boyfriend and I have no taste!"

My mother sighed. "You're not listening to me."

I heard her.

I just didn't like what she was saying.

We were fighting about an engagement ring for an engagement that hadn't even been proposed yet.

An hour later, my mother and I exchanged text messages:

> Cheer up. This is not a decision you have to make tonight. I appreciate you including me in all the wonderful things that are going on in your life. I do not mean to criticize. I just want you to have the best. I know everyone's tastes are different. I know you will make the right decision and get what you will be happy with. Will think twice before I speak from now on.

Guilt settled over my heart. Ring shopping was supposed to be fun. I texted my mother back:

> So much pressure—to get a ring that will impress my friends, impress America, even impress my mom. Pressure from my biological clock to get married while I can still have kids. Pressure to get married while my father is still alive to see me walk down the aisle. Don't forget the self-inflicted pressure of making 300 sandwiches. I haven't even gotten engaged and the challenges ahead of me are great.

Mom responded within a minute:

> You don't have to impress anyone when it comes to the ring, that's between you and him. . . . You have always put a lot of pressure on yourself. And bigger is not always better. When the time comes, discuss your budget and take it from there. I love you.

I sat back and took a few deep breaths. Then, I grabbed my iPad, opened the browser, and flipped to the "weddings and celebrations" category on Pinterest, nervously looking over my shoulder every few minutes in case E appeared from the office and caught me browsing for rings. This was only going to happen once in my life. I needed to enjoy it.

Saturday afternoon, E and I hit the jewelry shops. Oh, that rush I felt when we hopped on the subway to head toward Madison Avenue!

Our first stop was a crowded David Yurman boutique. The jewelry was organized on three floors. The first was your run-of-the-mill daywear pieces. Bracelets, necklaces, pendants. A security guard greeted us at the entrance, as did salespeople carrying glasses of champagne (yes, please!) to lubricate our palates. And our wallets.

E and I walked toward the back of the first floor to the winding staircase that took us to the second floor, where more turquoise and precious metals were in cases. The third floor was the bridal floor. A man wearing a black suit called for assistance through his headset. "Let me take you upstairs to see Jody. She'll show you some of our bridal jewelry," he said.

We climbed up the next set of stairs, and a perky blond woman was at the front near the elevator. She was wearing a black dress and heels; her glossy hair framed her full face, painted with red lipstick and black eyeliner. Her nails were freshly French manicured, and played up the large diamond engagement ring on her left ring finger.

"Hello, I'm Jody, I'll be helping you today. What is your name?"

We introduced ourselves.

"First, congratulations to the two of you. Now, do you know what you'd like?"

E spoke confidently. "We had a few things flagged, but we also wanted to try on a bunch of pieces and see how things looked up close." I smiled. I was so proud. Excited. Ready.

"Great!" Jody said with a wide smile. "Tell you what, why don't you get comfortable at that desk over there, and I'll pull a bunch of things for you?"

My smile formed deep creases in my cheeks so hard that my face hurt. We walked slowly, with intention, toward the back, where a glass desk was set up near a private office. On the desk were four more glasses of freshly poured champagne sitting on a tray and a rectangular plate of petits fours.

"Would you like anything to eat?" Jody offered. We grabbed another glass of champagne.

Jody brought out a tray of traditional rings. Princess cuts, emerald cuts, oval cut, halo settings, some with baguettes on the sides, others with pavé stones along the band. I tried them all on, admiring my left hand as I went.

I tried on stones of various sizes, most of them between one and three carats, in a variety of settings. We looked at two rings that E picked out. As Mom told me, they looked too costume-y to be engagement rings, but they were fantastic cocktail rings.

After trying on a dozen more rings, Jody handed me a square-cut halo setting to try on. It just felt right. It wasn't too big, but I appreciated its size. It was classic, and would go well with any band I chose. And, it was unquestionably an engagement ring. "What do you think, honey?"

"I like it," he said, reserved.

"I'll bring some more similar to this one," Jodi said, rushing off for more diamonds and more champagne.

Jody returned with more rings. "Then we have this one," she said, handing me a large princess-cut five-carat solitaire. It looked like something the celebrities and trophy wives I report on often wear. It sat on my thin ring finger like a boulder, an obstruction that would bang against the counter every time I reached for a pot or pan or loaf of bread in the refrigerator. I was sort of disgusted.

"I just don't know how I feel wearing this on the subway," I said.

"I agree with you," Jody said. "This is something you can upgrade to, once you're driving around Connecticut in your Jaguar."

RING SHOPPING—
CURRIED CHICKEN SALAD

The day after we went ring shopping, I took leftover roast chicken and made curried chicken salad sandwiches with toasted pecans. The seasoned nuts added a spicy crunch to the sandwich, and curry made the whole thing just a bit more interesting.

1 pat unsalted butter
⅓ cup pecans
1 teaspoon cinnamon
½ cup mayonnaise
1 teaspoon curry powder
½ teaspoon cayenne pepper
¼ tablespoon paprika
2 cups diced chicken
1 stalk celery, chopped
½ green apple, chopped
½ teaspoon black pepper
4 slices whole wheat bread

Toast the pecans: Melt the butter over low heat. Toss in the whole pecans and toast for 5 to 8 minutes, turning several times. Sprinkle with cinnamon halfway through cooking. Remove from the heat.

When cooled slightly, chop the pecans into rough pieces. Set aside.

Mix the mayonnaise, curry powder, cayenne pepper, and paprika in a small cup. Set aside.

In a large bowl, combine the chicken, celery, and apple. Add the toasted pecans. Then add the spiced mayo, and combine until well blended. Season with black pepper. Scoop chicken salad onto the bottom pieces of bread and finish with the other pieces of bread. Makes 2 sandwiches.

TWENTY-ONE

As my dad fought cancer, my mother had been his primary care-giver. Taking care of a sick partner or parent who is a day away from the end is no picnic. It hurts. It sucks. It's depressing.

And I didn't make it any better on Christmas.

I flew home ahead of E, who would meet me a few days later, on a rainy cold Saturday. I was delayed an hour because Delta Airlines lost the suitcase with all the Christmas gifts inside it somewhere between LaGuardia International Airport and Detroit Metropolitan Airport, and according to the ticket agent with better things to do than help me find said bag, it wasn't at LGA or in DTW. "I don't know where it is. Maybe just wait and see if it gets checked in later." Sure, I'll just wait and see . . . meanwhile I wished my family's gifts a happy holiday, wherever they were.

When I arrived home with only my one bag, I saw my father first. He was bundled in three layers of fleece, understandable for anyone living in Michigan in December. But he was colder than usual because he had less body weight to snuggle up in, plus chemo and radiation left him more sensitive to the elements. My mother came out of the bedroom and kissed me on the cheek.

I sat with Dad in his office for a bit, watching the news and assessing his health. I could see that his face was thinner. His eyes were tired, searching for peace among the hell that was contained in his tumor-stricken body. But yet, he still smiled. "What's the good gossip?" he asked.

Before I could respond with details on Leonardo DiCaprio's latest swimsuit-model girlfriend, Mom entered the office.

"You want something to eat?" my mother offered.

"No, I'm good. I'll probably make something for myself in a bit."

"Did you eat on the plane?"

"Not really, but I'll find something in a bit."

She stared at me, as if to will me off the couch and to the refrigerator.

"You hungry?" she asked Dad. He passed on food too. From the looks of his thin face, he did that often.

Mom looked at me again. "You sure?"

"Mom, I'll find something in a second."

She read the inventory of the food in her kitchen, as if I couldn't find everything in the cabinets myself, or fearing that I would find something and then put it back in the wrong place. "There's cookies, strawberries, Almond Joys, wheat bread, peanut butter, all in the cabinets. You know I don't know what you want, so . . ." She walked off frustrated.

One of the happy traditions Mom and I have during the holidays is baking Christmas cookies, and I wanted to start making some so we could cook while gossiping about the neighbors, my friends, Dad's health. I also thought I could make a few dessert sandwiches that would be ready in time for E's arrival, therefore adding to my sandwich count and getting that much closer to my 300 goal. I was willing to do the baking while she slept or sat down or took some rest. I followed her to the kitchen and started opening the cabinets underneath the countertop, assessing her pots and pans.

Instead, Mom seemed exhausted at the thought.

"Why make cookies when I have all these Oreos and Chips Ahoy here?" she asked.

Those had probably been in that cupboard since I was in school. "Because I want to make holiday cookies from scratch. Is that a problem?"

Somehow, the conversation turned into an argument. "For once, I just want us to have a good time and not bicker."

"Well, stop yelling at me!"

"I'm not yelling!"

"Yes you are!"

And then the waterworks began.

"I just try to be a good mother and take care of you and your father and your father can't even take care of himself and I have to be the mother and father and for thirty-seven years I've done everything and gotten no credit I can't believe this I do everything and I get no appreciation for it it's too much you blame me for everything I am tired of being the bully and the bad guy and the mean one why am I the mean one when I am just looking out for you! I am so tired.

"I am tired.

"I am tired!

"I am tired!!!!!!!!" she yelled.

Mom wept hard and angry, like she'd been angry for years and bitter and resentful and then angry at herself for feeling all of those feelings. I did not blame her.

"We are making his funeral arrangements in January."

I stopped breathing.

I threw both of my arms around her and smothered her head in my arms.

She cried and cried until my father scuffled toward the kitchen.

She wiped her face and slid to the bedroom and shut the door.

I left the baking supplies on the counter.

On Christmas Eve, E arrived. My parents were extremely excited about his arrival. Mom put on holiday music by the Temptations and Mariah Carey and James Brown, and had delicious sweet potatoes and vegetables in the oven cooking just as E pulled into the driveway.

My father, as ill as he was, brought in wood from outside to light a fire in the fireplace.

E's presence lightened the mood, because he was someone to focus on other than my father. Mom offered him a flurry of food when he arrived—chicken, a sandwich, bagels, cookies—but E quickly came to my father's office to sit with my dad and me as we watched television.

I didn't want to leave them alone for too long, not knowing if my father was tired or didn't feel like talking. But eventually, Mom summoned me out to the kitchen to help with dinner.

My mother had used all her strength to churn out an expansive Christmas Eve dinner comprised of the holiday staples—turkey, stuffing, sweet potatoes, vegetables, broccoli casserole, which E picked all of the broccoli out of (see Forbidden Foods list, page 29). We sat quietly around the kitchen table, shoveling tender turkey, crisp string beans, and chewy stuffing into our mouths, comforted by the taste of a home-cooked holiday meal. We focused on the food, that meal, and the four of us at the table. I tried hard to not think about whether this would be Dad's last time at the table with us.

After dinner, we retreated to the living room to watch a movie together, but since people were stuffed from the filling dinner, Dad and E turned in early. Mom and I followed closely afterward.

When we got ready for bed, I went into the bathroom to brush my teeth and change clothes, and Mom headed toward her bedroom—I could hear the creaking of the floor as she paced back and forth. Then I heard a faint knocking on the bathroom door, but when I didn't hear a voice behind it, I figured she went to sleep.

I opened the door a few minutes later and saw Mom sitting on the couch. "Psst!"

"What?"

"Come here. I want to tell you something."

I meandered over and plopped next to her on the couch. QVC was on the TV. I figured she was trying to show me some jewelry.

"Eric asked your dad for his blessing."

I covered my head with my hands and burst into tears.

"Isn't that great?" Mom asked, patting my head. "Cheer up, this is a good thing!"

My father never pressured E and me to hurry up and settle down. He never questioned E's loyalty to me. But he knew he didn't have much time left, and if he wasn't going to be around for a wedding, he at least wanted to know that E was committed to me. Dad just wanted to know someone was going to take care of his girl. And now, E had given him that assurance.

On Christmas, I appreciated every last minute with Dad. I sat at his feet opening gifts, helping him with his boxes before tearing open mine. My mother and I passed each other our things with a knowing look, delighting in the secret we'd shared late last night about E and my father. We took photos with bows stuck to our faces, and played our favorite Christmas carols—no Christmas in our house goes by without playing the Temptations' version of "Silent Night" on the stereo.

I shed tears like I'd never done before when E and I packed up the car and said our good-byes. Dad is usually the stoic one when I get in the car or head to the airport. But this time was different. He was weak. He couldn't talk. So he cried. And whispered, "I love you."

"Do you want me to stay? I can stay, Dad. I can go tomorrow," I told him.

"No, you go," he whispered. "People to see. You'll come back in a few months."

"I love you, Dad. I can stay and take care of you." Now heavy uncontrollable sobs broke up my speech.

"No, go, you don't have to take care of me," he said. "You have to take care of E now."

Even after he got up to grab a Kleenex, I just sat on the edge of the chair, crying into my own folded arms. I knew, and he knew, this was probably our last Christmas together.

. . .

E and I drove three hours to his parents' house for the rest of the holiday, arriving on Christmas night in time for dinner and to exchange gifts.

For Christmas, E's father, William, had 300-Sandwiches-branded fleece jackets made for us as a gag gift, our first piece of swag we had made for the website. He had some for E's cousins, his aunt, and anyone they were seeing for Christmas. He even had extras to send to my mother and father as gifts.

Renee churned out a lovely four-course dinner that included spinach salad with pecans and goat cheese, asparagus soup, and leg of lamb. We sat in the formal dining room as Renee presented each dish, the family catching up about work, weddings, family gossip, and which one of the 300 sandwiches was E's favorite.

The next day, we went to a local restaurant for brunch with the extended family—aunts, uncles, cousins. We laughed through a few rounds of drinks and lunch, then everyone caravaned back to E's parents' house for late-afternoon lounging. People may not have been hungry when they arrived, but after an hour of more wine and telling stories of holidays past around the fire, many got peckish.

"We've got roast chicken," Renee offered.

Somewhere between E reaching for the Scotch and William bringing in more firewood from outside and Aunt Sheryl telling a hilarious story about Uncle Gary leaving his car unlocked when he drove through downtown Detroit's municipal buildings for work ("That is NOT how we do it in the D," she warned), Renee pulled a whole bird out of the refrigerator, covered it with salt, pepper, and butter, and popped it in the oven. By the time the sun had sunk and the streetlights were on, that roast chicken was ready, placed on the stove still in its roasting pan, ready to be carved by any hungry family member.

While refilling our wine glasses, William asked, "So what's on the agenda for tomorrow?"

"We're going to Ahee's," E said.

Ahee Jewelers was a sixty-five-year-old family-run jewelry business in Grosse Pointe. It's the place anyone in Eastern Michigan with a well-paying job would go to buy jewelry for their wife, their children, their parents. Renee, who'd studied art in college, worked at Ahee's constructing bracelets, necklaces, and rings while pregnant with her son. "E would kick my belly under the table while I worked," she said.

The store was on Mack Avenue, a busy thoroughfare through the Grosse Pointes. On a holiday weekend, it was packed with couples browsing the dozens of jewelry counters that snaked through the airy boutique. There was plenty of elbow room to try on baubles, which a lot of women were doing as they looked at the colorful gemstones dancing underneath the glass cabinets. You could hear the low moans of customers cooing over the shiny pieces as the light danced over the stones.

Renee walked E and me into the jewelry store and was greeted by all the sales associates like a real VIP, as we waited for the general manager to walk us through the rings. Then from the back room, a tall, dark-haired, evenly tanned man named Peter greeted each one of us with a smile and a handshake.

"So what are we shopping for today?"

"Engagement rings," E said.

"Congratulations," Peter said. My face exploded into an open smile. I may not have known what I wanted, but I loved the discovery process.

Peter turned his attention toward me. "We have a wide selection of rings. Anything in particular you like? Or don't like?"

"Frankly, I'll try them all."

"Okay," Peter said. "Here's what we have." Peter waved his arm over four large sections of the display counter, then walked ten paces to the right, and waved his arm again. "All of these sections house our most popular ring settings. But this is by no means all we have. If you see something, or have something in mind you're looking to create, we can make it for you. Anything jump out at you that you want to try on first?"

"Um," I said, eyes wide, tongue wagging. "All of them."

E sighed heavily. "Let's start with this section, and work our way down." Renee stood between E and me as Peter slipped rings onto my ring finger.

Ring shopping with my future mother-in-law was different than browsing with E. I was conscious of not trying on the largest or most expensive rings, though I had done so while ring shopping alone. The kind of ring I chose demonstrated what type of spendthrift I was. The larger the diamond, the more likely she would think I would be the materialistic wife who demanded a bigger house on the cul-de-sac, with the three-car garage filled with two gas-guzzling import SUVs. But if I chose something modest, Renee could see that I treasured something that was thoughtful and unique, no matter what the size. That would make me look like a more agreeable daughter-in-law, right?

"What about this one?" E said.

He pointed to an octagon-shaped ring with a bezel halo setting. One large stone was surrounded by dozens of smaller stones around it and on the band. I had never seen a setting like this before, and I had a feeling I never would again on any other woman. It looked both old and modern at one glance.

"I love this one," I told E. I tried on other rings, and took more photos of rings on my finger with my iPhone to send to my mother. But I tried on that unique octagonal ring three more times.

"Okay, now . . . go away." E shooed his mother and me away from the counter so he could speak with Peter in private. Renee and I walked around the store together, looking in the glass cases, cooing at different pieces. I silently prayed that I wasn't too outlandish with my ring choices.

"Isn't this exciting?" she said.

"Absolutely," I replied. Then, I tried to make it seem like I wasn't in this just for the ring, that I was worried about E's budget as much as he was. "But I don't want him to go broke buying a ring for me."

"I wouldn't worry about that," Renee replied. "This is fun for him too."

. . .

Back in New York, New Year's Day brought new energy. E and I celebrated with friends at dinner out at Le Bilboquet on the Upper East Side, a favorite of uptown Europeans who favor Loro Piana and Jaguars and summers in the south of France. Dinner was more of a disco supper, where dance music was cranked up loudly while people snacked on steak frites and Cajun chicken, washing it all down with champagne. When midnight hit, the waitstaff pushed the tables back and patrons shimmied and danced in the middle of the restaurant. E and I donned silly hats, kissed at midnight, and told each other how grateful we were to have another year together. "To many more," I told him.

The next day, we were eager to get started on our goals for the year. Work out regularly. Travel more, eat better, start using that college-level Spanish I'd all but abandoned since studying abroad. Get engaged. Make a few more sandwiches.

I called my mother. A huge snowstorm was stomping across the Midwest and headed to the East Coast, so I wanted to check in. "What are you up to?"

"Just looking on the computer."

"For what?"

"Nothing, Stef."

I knew that was not the truth.

"What are you looking at, sandwiches?"

"No, Stef." She paused, wanting to hold back, but remembering that she promised me she wouldn't do that anymore. "I'm looking up what happens when you take someone off of chemotherapy."

"You mean Dad?"

"Yes."

"The doctors took him off chemo?"

"Yes."

"Why?"

"Because it isn't working, Stef. It's just not working."

"But he's already beat the previous six to nine months to live diagnosis," I said. "How is it not working?"

"It's not stopping the cancer from spreading."

My diaphragm sunk heavily into my abdomen. "So now what?"

"Now nothing, Stef."

I couldn't comprehend that.

"The doctors have already said they can't do surgery, and they can't put him on any clinical trials, because there are none he qualifies for right now. All he can do is try to relieve the pain as much as possible, and . . . wait."

Waiting was something I couldn't do.

"Okay. Is there anything I can do?"

"Do you want to say hello to him?"

"Yes."

He came to the phone and could barely get out a hello. "I'm tired, Stef. I'm going to lay down for a second."

"Okay, Dad. I love you."

"Love you too. Good night."

It was 3:15 P.M.

I worked through whatever emotions I had from that conversation by making dinner. I made turkey burgers, but I didn't even have the energy to shake on any seasoning to make sure they didn't taste like cotton cushions. I didn't even count them on the blog. After we washed the bland burgers down with some red wine, E and I snuggled up to watch *March of the Penguins,* and watched how the families of the black-and-white birds gather together to protect and feed themselves through a harsh winter. I remember how Mom and Dad and I had all sat around and watched this movie for the first time together, a few Christmases ago.

"I'm heartbroken," I told E.

He held me until I stopped crying, just as the credits came across the screen at the end of the movie.

HOLIDAY MISADVENTURES—
MINT CHOCOLATE CHIP ICE CREAM SANDWICHES

When I finally got around to making the Christmas cookies, I made these mint chocolate chip numbers, adapted from Foodess.com. It was the first cookie I learned to bake from scratch without my mother's assistance, when I was forced to contribute to a bake sale at a job in my early twenties. When my father caught a glimpse of them coming out of the oven, he joked that they looked like "Christmas turds," before inhaling two of them. These might not have been the prettiest cookie sandwiches, but they were damn tasty. My father ate more than a few of those "turds" before Christmas was over.

butter or cooking spray
2 cups all-purpose flour
1 teaspoon baking soda
½ teaspoon baking powder
½ teaspoon salt
1 cup dark chocolate cocoa
1 cup unsalted butter, softened
1¾ cups sugar
2 eggs
2 tablespoons peppermint extract
1 cup semisweet chocolate chips
1 pint vanilla ice cream

Preheat the oven to 350 degrees. Grease baking sheets with butter or cooking spray.

In a medium bowl, thoroughly combine the flour, baking soda, baking powder, salt, and cocoa. Set aside.

In a large bowl, blend the butter and sugar until light and fluffy. Add the eggs and peppermint extract. Stir in the flour mixture until well blended. Fold in the chocolate chips.

Spoon the dough by tablespoons onto the baking sheets, leaving 2 inches between each. Press down slightly to spread out the dough into a sphere. Bake about 10 minutes, or until the tops are just set.

Remove the cookies from the sheets and let cool on a wire rack.

When cool, scoop a teaspoon-size scoop of ice cream onto a cookie, top with another, and enjoy. Makes about 2 dozen sandwiches.

sandwich

#213

GOOD LUCK IN 2014—HOPPIN' JOHN WRAPS

Black-eyed peas are said to bring you good luck on New Year's Day. If you have leftovers, make these Hoppin' John Wraps with black-eyed peas, greens, and white rice.

½ pound dried black-eyed peas
⅓ pound bacon, chopped into small pieces
2 garlic cloves, minced
4 scallions, chopped
1 small green bell pepper, chopped
1 stalk celery, chopped
2 to 3 sprigs thyme
1 teaspoon black pepper
½ teaspoon cayenne pepper
1 teaspoon red pepper flakes
½ teaspoon Old Bay seasoning
2 bay leaves
3 to 4 cups water
2 pieces roll-up flatbread
Kale, collard greens, or Boston bibb lettuce (optional)
½ cup cooked rice

Make the Hoppin' John: The night before, or some 6 hours before you're going to cook, soak the peas in water. Rinse and drain. In a large pan, cook the bacon slowly over medium-low heat. When the bacon gets nice and crisp, add the garlic and cook on medium-high heat for a minute. Stir in the scallions, peppers, and celery and sauté for 5 minutes. Add the black-eyed peas, thyme, black pepper, cayenne pepper, red pepper flakes, and Old Bay seasoning. Stir to combine. Add the bay leaves and pour in the water. Stir, cover, and simmer on low heat for 30 minutes to an hour, until the peas are tender, but not mushy.

Drain the water, remove the bay leaves and thyme sprigs, stir, and taste. You can add or alter spice as needed (I add more pinches of red pepper flakes to finish the dish before I make sandwiches).

When ready to assemble the sandwiches, warm the flatbreads over medium heat in a nonstick pan for a few seconds on each side. On each piece of bread, stack greens if using, rice, and the Hoppin' John. Fold each flatbread in, top and bottom first, then the sides. Cut in half to serve. Makes 2 sandwiches.

sandwich

#210

TEAM EFFORT—EGGNOG FRENCH TOAST SANDWICHES

French toast makes a great breakfast for the masses. Cognac makes it even more holiday appropriate.

Eggnog
6 eggs, separated
¾ cup sugar
2 cups milk
2 cups heavy cream
⅓ cup bourbon
¼ cup cognac
¼ cup peppermint liqueur (gives the 'nog a real Christmas feel)

French toast sandwiches
½ teaspoon nutmeg
½ teaspoon cinnamon
½ teaspoon pumpkin pie spice
4 slices brioche or day-old wheat bread
2 tablespoons apple butter
1 cup raspberries
1 cup blackberries
sprinkle of confectioners' sugar

Make the eggnog: In a large metal bowl, beat the egg yolks until thick and pale. Slowly beat in the sugar. Whisk in the milk and cream. Mix in the bourbon, cognac, and peppermint liqueur. Cover and refrigerate for up to a day.

Right before serving, add the egg whites. Beat the whites (or mix with an immersion blender, which is much easier) until stiff peaks form. Fold the whites into the eggnog. If you're serving it to drink, sprinkle with nutmeg. If you're only using eggnog for the French toast, add the egg whites just before using the batter for the French toast, using the same method.

Make the French toast: Stir nutmeg, cinnamon, and pumpkin pie spice into the eggnog. Dip the bread into the mixture to evenly coat each piece.

In a medium nonstick pan on medium heat, cook the battered bread until browned, 2 to 3 minutes on each side, flipping once. Remove from heat. Lay out the French toast and smooth apple butter on the bottom pieces. (Nutella is also good here, if you're feeling really indulgent.) Stack with berries and finish with another slice of French toast. Sprinkle with confectioners' sugar. Cut in half to serve. Makes 2 sandwiches.

TWENTY-TWO

> Need to make more sandwiches.
> I want to give you away at your
> wedding. Love you both, stay warm.

—*Text from Dad*

I met E for dinner one night, shortly after the holidays had passed. He held my hands. "I want to ask you something," he said. "What if we fly home, and we get your parents and my parents together, and we get married, for your dad?"

"WHAT?"

"Not a legal ceremony, but more ceremonial. And we won't tell anyone. It would allow your dad to see us get married, even if whoever marries us wouldn't be official," E suggested.

"When?" I asked.

"How about next weekend?" E asked.

A bit rushed, I thought.

"Look, your dad said he wanted to walk you down the aisle, and I want to give that to him. We'll keep it super-casual. We don't even have to go to the courthouse, we'll do some quick vows, and then we'll have a simple brunch and call it a day. We'll order Chinese food afterward! And people can wear jeans or flannel shirts or whatever he wants to wear. Easy. What do you say?"

He was able to plan this faster than he planned a weekend snow-boarding trip upstate.

"Are you just doing this because of my father?"

"No, I'm doing this because I want to. I want to give your father that opportunity to walk you down the aisle."

I was overwhelmed by the gesture. But was E ready to be married?

"You want to marry me right now? This weekend?"

He looked me in the eyes. "Well, you've still got sandwiches to make—a deal is still a deal—but why not?"

But I knew E wasn't ready to be married. Not like this. Not rushed. Not without time to plan out the details. Time for him to buy some decent dress shoes to go with his suit. To notify our friends and apply for a marriage license. And certainly not without a long enough engagement to preside over the planning of the above.

My parents agreed.

"Dad just wants you two to be happy. That's all he needs. He doesn't need a wedding. He just wants to know you'll be happy.

"We shouldn't make any plans right now," said Mom. "Who knows what could happen between now and then?"

TWENTY-THREE

My mother called me around noon on a Thursday, with a chirpiness in her voice, as if she was hiding a secret. "Hi! Whatcha doing?"

"Looking up recipes for pulled pork," I told her. It was thirty degrees out in New York City, and a snowstorm that already dumped ten inches of snow in Michigan was headed our way. It was perfect weather for warm, sweet molasses-flavored meat on a toasted bun. "What's up?"

"I'm about to leave the house for the first time in five days," she joked. "I have to get some groceries. Looks like we're having company."

"What do you mean?"

"Renee called me today. She said she would like to come to our house on Monday and meet us. And I agreed."

My stomach dropped. The parents were about to meet.

"Renee offered to come Friday but we looked at the weather and said that wouldn't work, as it's about to snow here again. Sunday looked like a better day."

"Is she coming alone?"

"I think William is coming as well."

"Does Eric know this is happening?"

"I don't know," Mom said.

Eric had mentioned to me the night before that he hadn't spoken to his mother yet this week. He had no clue the families were about to have a meet-and-greet. "Well. Wow."

E's parents knew my father was ill, and getting worse. They were eager to meet my parents and spend time with my father before it was too late, so they volunteered to drive three hours across the state in the snow and cold and whatever else Mother Nature had to throw at them in order to meet my parents.

I digested the image of what this meeting would be like. I thought about what could happen. What if my mother embarrassed me? What if my dad's illness was too much for them to handle? What if they didn't like our house, given its location miles away from civilization? What if they didn't like each other? What if they didn't play nicely in the proverbial sandbox? Would this mean E wouldn't propose? Or would be discouraged by his parents from proposing?

More important, "What are you going to cook?" I asked my mother.

"I don't know." Mom pondered. "I have no idea what she likes, or what William would want, or if we're going to go out. But I do need something 'cooking' in case they want to stay in too."

I thought about what I would cook if we had company coming over on a cold snowy winter's day. Maybe something in a Crock-Pot? You can prepare meatballs before they arrive, and they can cook for six hours or so, without having to stand over an oven. "Hmm, what about venison meatballs? Those are good, I like to have things going in a slow cooker. Then they can be appetizers or main course."

"I'm out of venison. I was thinking maybe chicken cacciatore. Or a nice roast."

Roast. Roast was Mom's Sunday go-to dinner. Always in a roasting pot, with potatoes and carrots, served with thick gravy on Sundays with a baked potato, in time for *60 Minutes* to be broadcast on our family television.

"I'm sure whatever you make, they'll enjoy," I said.

E and I were in Lake Placid snowboarding the day his parents were due to arrive at my parents' house. Snowboarding was something we enjoyed together, a sport that we were both equally skilled in. Though the summers might be for chasing wind around the world so E could kitesurf, the winters were for riding the slopes in tandem, only taking a break for lunch and an occasional hot chocolate.

I texted my parents a "good luck and let me know how it goes" message. I hoped my parents would be merciful and send me updates via text so that I didn't sit around all day worrying what embarrassing stories about me they were sharing with my future in-laws.

Despite my texts,

How's it going?

Did they make it there safely?

Are you eating?

I got radio silence.

"I hope they're having a good time," I told E.

"I'm sure they're fine," he said. "What do you expect, hair pulling?"

We continued up the ski lift and whizzed down the white slopes together.

E and I drove back from Lake Placid at sunset, the rolling hills covered in snow whizzing by our windows. A "Quiet Storm" playlist of soulful R&B hits from the '70s and '80s rotated through songs on our car stereo: Smokey Robinson to Teena Marie to the Gap Band to Aretha Franklin to Michael McDonald.

E, a die-hard fan of the Rolling Stones, didn't know what the "quiet storm" was until I told him about the radio format from the '70s and '80s on urban stations that would kick in on Sunday nights around 9:00. Smokey Robinson released his song "Quiet Storm" in 1975, which has an unmistakable high-pitched organ intro that got many a bell-bottomed and Afro-wearing couple in the baby-making mood, if you know what I'm saying. That song inspired disc jockeys in DC to play a set of slow jams during their late Sunday-night set, and soon, urban stations across the country played Luther Vandross and Anita Baker and Peabo Bryson tracks on Sunday evenings as a romantic wind-down to the weekend.

These songs were the tunes of my parents' day, of their courtship, songs that played in the car as they drove back from dinner, or at the house party they went to with friends, or that they played at home on their stereo while slow dancing or, following in the words of Marvin Gaye, "getting it on."

On Sunday nights driving back from Michigan to Chicago after a weekend at the lake during my childhood, the Quiet Storm was always on the radio in the car while Dad drove, Mom sat in the front seat, and I splayed across the back seat fading in and out of consciousness.

When I explained what the Quiet Storm was to E, he quickly downloaded the most extensive playlist he could find. He eagerly turned on the music while we drove back from our various road trips on Sunday nights. When a real good slow jam came on, like "Yearning for Your Love," by the Gap Band, E reached over from the driver's side, and grabbed my hand, holding it until I looked up and then blowing me a kiss. Like Sunday brunches at Grandma's or recipes for chocolate chip cookies, Sunday-night Quiet Storm playlists were a Smith family tradition E and I were keeping alive.

While I sat in the passenger seat, wondering how the meeting of the parents went, my phone beeped. It was a text message from William.

He sent a photo of my father and him together, standing in my living room, sharing smiles. I showed E. They looked like they'd known each other for a lifetime.

I had another text message from Renee. She sent me three photos of herself playing with my old Cabbage Patch dolls my mother had on display in her office.

> Nya nya! All mine!

she wrote.
I texted back.

> Glad to see Jeanette is sharing her toys with others.

I guess the kids did play well in the sandbox.

THE CLASSICS

Within my recipe box of 300 Sandwiches, I made several versions of traditional sandwiches. Ham and cheese. Monte Cristo. French dip. The classics. Sometimes I did them more than once, adhering to the rules and the Forbidden Foods list. Here are some 300 "classics."

STEPHANIE SMITH

THE MONTE CRISTO

I made this one right after Hurricane Sandy, which landed just before Halloween, in honor of New Jersey governor Chris Christie. We were out of town for the hurricane, but we witnessed how Christie was praised for his leadership during the crisis and cleanup. One of the things he did was make sure to reschedule Halloween to November 5 so kids could go trick-or-treating, since they missed doing so during the storm. Gotta respect a man who is looking out for the kids.

1 egg
⅓ cup milk
salt and pepper
4 slices bread
2 tablespoons Dijon mustard
sliced ham (as much as you want)
sliced turkey (ditto)
sliced Swiss cheese (ditto again)
2 tablespoons unsalted butter
confectioners' sugar
2 tablespoons red or black currant jam

In a shallow baking dish or bowl, whisk together the egg and milk. Season with salt and pepper. Assemble the sandwiches on a work surface: Lay two pieces of bread out and slather on Dijon mustard. Then layer equal portions of turkey and ham on each sandwich. Next add the cheese, and finish the sandwiches with the other slices of bread, assembling each sandwich.

Melt the butter in a medium nonstick pan on low to medium heat. Carefully hold each sandwich in both hands and coat top, bottom, and sides in the egg mixture. Place the sandwiches in the pan and fry for about 4 minutes on each side, flipping once. Remove from the pan and sprinkle confectioners' sugar on top. Serve with a side of red or black currant jam. Makes 2 sandwiches.

sandwich

#16

BACON, LETTUCE, AND "I HATE TOMATO" SANDWICH

Note the clever use of a peach in place of forbidden tomatoes.

4 to 5 slices bacon
1 medium peach, sliced
2 pinches sugar
2 tablespoons mayonnaise
1 teaspoon Sriracha sauce
1 teaspoon lime juice
salt and pepper
4 slices sourdough bread
1 cup frisée or arugula

Fry the bacon until crisp. Drain on a paper-towel-lined plate. Sprinkle the peach slices with sugar. Set aside.

In a small bowl, stir together the mayonnaise, Sriracha sauce, lime juice, and salt and pepper.

Toast the bread. Spread mayonnaise mixture on slices of bread. On the bottom pieces, layer frisée or arugula, then slices of peaches, and top with strips of bacon. Finish with the other pieces of bread and cut in half to serve. Makes 2 sandwiches.

sandwich

#185

CRAVING NEW YORK—PASTRAMI AND PROVOLONE ON RYE

I discovered my love for the legendary Katz's Deli in New York through this sandwich. It is the place to get a pastrami on rye sandwich. They give you, like, a pound of beef on each order, so it seems. I bought a pound of beef for my own sandwich—and then promptly went back for another pound the next day.

3 tablespoons mayonnaise

2 tablespoons honey mustard

1 tablespoon horseradish

black pepper

2 slices rye bread

4 to 5 slices pastrami

2 slices provolone cheese

1 tablespoon unsalted butter

In a small bowl, stir together the mayonnaise, honey mustard, horseradish, and black pepper and set aside. Lay out the bread and smooth the spicy mayonnaise on the bottom piece, then add the meat and cheese. Finish with the other piece of bread. Melt the butter in a nonstick pan, then place sandwich in the pan to warm, flipping once. When the cheese is melted, remove from heat and slice in half to serve. Makes 1 sandwich.

sandwich

#8

THE LOBSTER ROLL

When I first started cooking, E had to do everything with the lobster—buy it, cook it, crack it open, and get the meat out. After I got comfortable, I graduated to tossing the live critters into the boiling water like a big girl.

2 pounds cooked lobster meat
⅓ cup mayonnaise
2 tablespoons lemon juice
⅓ cup chopped celery
½ teaspoon salt
1 teaspoon black pepper
pinch of Old Bay seasoning
4 hot dog buns
1 to 2 tablespoons unsalted butter
chopped chives (optional)

Chop the steamed fresh lobster meat into small pieces. Place in a large bowl and stir in the mayonnaise, lemon juice, celery, salt, pepper, and Old Bay seasoning. Combine until the lobster meat is covered in the seasoned mayo mix. Cover and put in fridge until ready to serve.

Toast the buns: Melt the butter in a nonstick pan, and brown the buns face down until toasty. Spoon lobster mixture into buns. Top with cut-up chives as garnish if desired. Makes 4 lobster rolls.

HOLD THE PICKLES—CUBAN SANDWICH

1 small baguette or roll
2 tablespoons olive oil
2 tablespoons yellow mustard
3 or 4 slices ham
3 or 4 slices turkey
2 or 3 slices Swiss cheese
1 large dill pickle, sliced
black pepper

Slice the baguette or roll in half. Drizzle olive oil on the outside, and slather mustard on both halves on the inside. On the bottom, stack the ham, turkey, Swiss cheese, and pickle. Season to taste with black pepper, and finish with the other piece of bread. Toast in a panini machine or in a nonstick pan with a sandwich press. It's done when it is toasted on the outside and the cheese is melting. Makes 1 sandwich.

"MILES OF LOVE"—CHICKEN PARMESAN SANDWICH

After I ran the New York Half Marathon, I ate this tasty sandwich because I was starving! This is breaded cheesy chicken tomato-y goodness right here.

1 tablespoon olive oil
½ cup unseasoned bread crumbs
¼ cup Italian herbs or herbes de Provence
¼ cup dried oregano
pinch of kosher salt
½ teaspoon black pepper
1 egg
4 large boneless, skinless chicken breasts (about 1 pound)
4 or 5 slices fresh mozzarella
1 24-ounce jar marinara sauce
2 tablespoons chopped parsley
1 to 2 tablespoons red pepper flakes
1 baguette
¼ cup shredded Parmesan cheese (optional)

Coat the bottom of a Crock-Pot with olive oil.

In a medium bowl, combine the bread crumbs, Italian (or French) herbs, oregano, salt, and pepper. In another medium bowl, beat the egg. Coat the chicken breasts first with egg, then dip them in the bread crumb mixture to cover the chicken pieces thoroughly. Place the breasts in the Crock-Pot.

Layer slices of mozzarella on top of the chicken. Pour the marinara sauce on top. Cover and cook 6 to 8 hours on low to medium heat or 4 hours on high heat. A half hour from completion, sprinkle the parsley and red pepper flakes on top.

When ready to serve, toast the baguette and cut into 4-to-6-inch sandwich-size pieces. Lay the chicken breast on the bread and top with a heaping spoonful of sauce. Top with grated Parmesan as a garnish, if you like. Makes 4 sandwiches.

TWENTY-FOUR

Friend to me: "Has he asked you to slow down the sandwiches?"

Me to friend: "He hasn't encouraged me to speed up!"

I started to dabble in weddings at about sandwich #220. I flagged wedding bands and engagement rings I liked on Pinterest and browsed bridal sites to look at other people's real weddings, studying different options for decor, table settings, and invitations. I held on to a complimentary copy of *Brides* magazine that fell on my desk at work instead of passing it off to someone else's cubicle. I read stories from start to finish about celebrity engagements, looking at the woman's left hand to see how large the ring was and evaluate if something of that size and shape would look good on me. I took in details of the proposal, the history of the relationship, and compared it to mine. I was really becoming that girl who was about to get engaged. And I enjoyed it.

Then I went full-on wedding crazy.

Everywhere I looked, people were getting engaged. Friends were posting photos of themselves draping their left hand over their leg or shoulder or over their new fiancé's shoulder on their Facebook and Twitter and Instagram feeds. In three months, I wrote about no fewer than twelve weddings and/or engagements, including two MTV celebrities, that guy from the *Hangover* movies, two former cast members of the Real Housewives franchise, one member of

Mötley Crüe, perennial bachelor George Clooney, AND one of his ex-girlfriends.

After writing about weddings, reading about them in magazines and my social media feed, and seeing coverage of celebrity weddings on every channel that cable had to offer, and with my father's health getting worse, I too wanted to be engaged. I wanted my ring, and I wanted it before I prepared sandwich #300.

With 80-some sandwiches left, I figured I could bang out the remaining sandwiches in a few months. Maybe I'd throw some parties, or break the rules and do a series of peanut butter and jelly or tea sandwiches to make dozens at a time, thus exponentially growing my sandwich tally per meal. I could game the system.

"You know, I think I'm going to double-time my sandwich production," I told E while he cooked dinner, again. On the menu: arctic char, with roasted cumin-and-honey carrots and pickled radishes.

"When do you think you're going to get to 300?" E asked.

"Hopefully by June first."

"Well, then, you have two months."

"Or earlier!" I said.

"No, you should just keep at your same pace," E said.

"Why?"

"Because I said so."

"But you said sandwich three hundred!"

"I also said it's not a wise thing to rush it."

"I don't see why I should have to wait," I told E.

Silence. He sliced vegetables aggressively, stewing in silence, avoiding my gaze.

And then I wondered—what if E wasn't ready to propose?

I figured he would be ready to pop the question when I hit #300, which, at an average pace of three sandwiches a week, would mean sometime in the spring. But what if he wasn't? What if, after dating and living with me through 200-some sandwiches, he got cold feet? The emotional turmoil of dealing with my sick father, or the pressure from America to propose after exposing our relationship all over the

Internet, or our families, or our arguments over who did the dishes last or who was going to buy the next round of groceries, or his own reasons or fears or insecurities could make him scared to pop the question.

I had never thought about what would happen if he didn't propose. I assumed he would—just at his own pace. I didn't care what sandwich I was on when E chose to propose. Sure, it could be 300, or at 275 or 301.

But I could be wrong.

After two minutes of chopping, E put the knife down, and told me the real reason he didn't want me to rush the process.

"Because rings don't get made overnight, nor do they get paid for overnight!"

I just stood there staring at him.

"Actually, I take that back. Go as fast as you like, dear. Finish next week! It's just that that diamond will be the size of a Grape-Nut."

I retreated in my chair, slinking back, and forced myself to think about something else other than getting married.

One more Facebook post about one more friend getting engaged was all the kryptonite needed to turn me from a rational partner in an otherwise healthy adult relationship into Bridezilla. At work, the latest copy of *Brides* magazine was still sitting in my stack of mail. I had not discarded it, because I thought by now I would be flipping through that book to research an actual wedding—mine. I sat at my desk and took ten minutes to flip through the pages of wedding dresses and decor. The fantasies of destination weddings and bridal showers and honeymoons constructed themselves in my brain. Beaches. White dresses. Surf and turf.

I turned to Page Six deputy editor Ian Mohr, with whom in a span of the nine-plus hours we spend together each day I converse about everything from Public Enemy to Kim Kardashian to David Byrne in one go, in addition to the columns' worth of gossip we churn out for the *Post*. Ian, married with a child, looks like Clark Kent, with his black-rimmed glasses, short dark hair, and Paul Smith/Brooks Brothers layered Brooklyn style. But get him talking about '80s and '90s hip-hop and you'd think he grew up in the Marcy Houses housing projects in the apartment next to Jay Z.

"Ian, I can't take it anymore," I said. "I want to be married and engaged and it's never going to happen!"

Gentle Peabody-looking Ian waved his finger at me. "Stop."

"But . . ."

"No." He put his hand out to me. "I'm going to stop you right there. Stop. Don't. No. Don't. Stop."

"But, just listen."

"No. Because you're going to drive him crazy, and yourself crazy. And, you might ruin whatever surprise or plans he may have in store for you."

"But I just . . ."

Ian held his hand up and looked away. "Look, I'm married. I almost didn't get married because my wife almost did the same thing you're about to do. She went crazy thinking I wasn't going to propose. But she didn't know I was working on designing her ring, getting the antique stone from her aunt, having her jewelry designer friend craft it for two months. And why would she? It's supposed to be a surprise! So just chill out and let life happen. You don't know when it will happen. But I'm sure, if he's let you go two hundred some sandwiches deep into your relationship, he's planning to propose."

My pulse was racing. I folded up the *Brides* magazine. "But what if . . ."

"Stop. You're about to wreck everything if you don't just stay cool. You cannot think about this. Just be cool."

I, the gossip reporter who knew the inner workings of people's lives often before they knew the inner workings of their own lives, had a hard time comprehending this theory of "letting life happen."

I couldn't manipulate when E would be ready to propose. I couldn't beat it out of him. I couldn't beg for it. I couldn't force it. The sandwiches were only going to encourage him so far. Really, it all came down to when E was ready.

He held all the cards.

All I held were some sandwiches.

Damn.

"Okay," I told Ian. "I'll chill out."

I put the magazine back on my desk, and Ian and I went back to gossiping about other people's weddings.

A week later, I was hyperventilating again.

Pulled pork was something I usually made on the weekends, letting the meat slowly steam for a good six hours in a mixture of vinegar, spices, honey, and barbecue sauce until ready. That is, until we got a pressure cooker. With that marvel of technology, gifted to us for E's birthday in April, we could churn out tender pulled pork in an hour, tender artichokes in fifteen minutes, and beets in a blazingly fast twelve minutes.

After one night's dinner of pulled pork sandwiches with fried shallots and scallions, I used the leftovers for pulled pork gyros with roasted yellow tomatoes and homemade red cabbage slaw.

Right around when we were devouring those pulled pork gyros for lunch, I had to write one more story about one more couple getting engaged. The man, a real estate tycoon. His fiancée? A model. The couple flew on private planes to vacations in St. Barth and owned multiple homes. I was happy for the happy couple, until I got home later that day and started filling E in on the details—how the guy proposed (private jet to Aspen, champagne and five-carat ring on tarmac), who designed the ring (Harry Winston), what she said (yes, of course), and where the wedding will be (they're thinking Gstaad, since they're avid skiers, but might do Anguilla, where he owns property).

Then I ignored all of Ian's wise words and transformed into Bridezilla once again.

I had more than enough anecdotal evidence that with the latest story of yet another titan of New York business getting engaged, *everyone* was now engaged. Even George Freaking Clooney, perpetual bachelor, who dated cocktail waitresses and former WWE wrestlers for years with no intention of getting married, finally got engaged to a smoking-hot, thirty-six-year-old international lawyer he'd been dating FOR ONLY SIX MONTHS.

Jealousy took over my brain, and I, Bridezilla Smith, blurted out something I shouldn't have said: *"Everyone's getting engaged but me!"*

E stabbed the cutting board, leaving the knife upright.

"Really? *Everyone!?* Don't you think you've got that kinda wrapped up by now, with me tearing my hair out researching diamonds and saving every dollar I have?" He glared at me.

E sucked his teeth in frustration. "You know what? I'm sorry if life didn't work out for you, love. Why don't you put on a little dress, go to a nightclub tonight, and find some hedge-funder that'll walk you to Harry Winston and put it on his black card!?"

Oh, I had done it now.

"Or, better yet, you want me to do it here in the kitchen?"

"I . . . no."

E stormed out of the kitchen.

I had done a horrible thing. And I couldn't take it back.

A few hours later, E sent me an email, with no subject line:

You know, you really play the world's smallest violin sometimes. Yes, everybody's getting engaged . . . except for you. And everybody files in private jets . . . except for you. And everybody gets to travel to far-away places . . . except for . . . oh no, wait, we do that too. I think being too exposed to people you write about in Page Six or follow on Instagram is warping your sense of reality.

There it was, straight from my potential fiancé's lips . . . or fingers. I wanted to live like a Kardashian and was upset that I wasn't.

Hey, you could be marrying a grandfather who doesn't want kids, or dating a cook who doesn't cook for you, or some banker who works 100 hours weekly and then cheats on you. It sounds like your life is pretty okay to me, you with your man who loves you, who cooks for you constantly, in a nice apartment in a tony neighborhood driving a nice car and going on vacations to places most people never see in their lifetime.

I wrote him back:

You're absolutely right that being exposed to the 1 percent all the time gives me a skewed perspective of normal. I completely admit it's a problem. It doesn't mean I love you less. But I do feel that I deserve just as grand a future for myself.

E, to me:

The 1 percent? You have to be kidding me. More like the 0.25%. What exactly have these fiancées of wealthy guys done to get to the positions that they are in other than basically being born and having some charm? And George Clooney didn't pick a boring run-of-the-mill Pilates or inverted yoga instructor or whatever. . . . He picked a high-powered independent human rights lawyer. Boom. He's also 52 and doesn't need a calendar year+ to save for a ring. Ta da!

And by the way, emulating the life of those you cover would be working your ass off till exhaustion, getting up at 6 A.M. and working till 3 A.M. 7 days a week. Or maybe you want to emulate a kept Hamptons housewife? Is that what you want? The life of a Real Housewife? Because I'm not into that sorta girl. NOT. IN. TO. IT. AT. ALL.

He was right. I wouldn't propose to myself.

BEET PESTO AND ROASTED
ARTICHOKE GRILLED CHEESE

I got really good at making condiments during this journey, specifically pestos. This beet pesto was one of my masterpieces—a bright purple, creamy spread that went well with veggie sandwiches. I paired it with artichoke and fresh parsley for this grilled cheese.

1 artichoke
1 or 2 garlic cloves
I teaspoon lemon juice
salt and pepper
2 tablespoons olive oil
2 slices bread
4 to 5 slices Monterey Jack cheese
2 tablespoons beet pesto (see page 128)
1 tablespoon chopped fresh Italian parsley
1 tablespoon butter

Roast the artichoke: Preheat the oven to 425 degrees. Cut off the artichoke stem and ⅓ of the top. Push the garlic down into the flower. Drizzle with lemon juice and sprinkle with salt and pepper. Drizzle olive oil on aluminum foil and a bit on top of the artichoke, and wrap artichoke in aluminum foil. Roast for an hour and 15 minutes and remove from the oven to cool. Strip off the leaves until left with the heart. Cut it into small pieces.

Assemble the sandwich: On one piece of bread, lay the cheese slices. Spread the beet pesto on the other piece of bread. Sprinkle the cheese side with the artichoke hearts and parsley. Top with the other piece of bread (beet pesto on the inside, of course). Melt the butter in a medium nonstick pan on medium heat and brown the sandwich on both sides until the cheese is melted. Slice in half and serve. Makes 1 sandwich.

PRESSURE COOKER PULLED PORK SANDWICH

Somewhere in between the dramas over everyone else's engagements, we celebrated E's birthday. His mother got him a pressure cooker,* so we used it to flash-cook foods in minutes that would normally take hours. Pulled pork, which normally takes half a day to make, was the first thing we tried out, adapted from an America's Test Kitchen recipe. Dinner was served in an hour, and we had sandwiches for days afterward.

¼ cup turbinado sugar
2 tablespoons sweet paprika
2 tablespoons cumin
1 tablespoon chili powder
1 tablespoon cinnamon
1 teaspoon salt
1 teaspoon black pepper
4-to-5-pound pork butt or shoulder
1 cup apple cider
1 cup water
½ cup ketchup
1 tablespoon liquid smoke
1 cup vegetable oil
1 shallot, sliced thin
2 scallions, chopped
6 to 8 hoagie rolls
extra barbecue sauce (optional)

*Read the instructions on your pressure cooker before cooking. We skimmed them because we're overgrown children who just want to play with toys before reading the manuals. But please, cook responsibly.

In a small bowl, put the sugar, sweet paprika, cumin, chili powder, cinnamon, salt, and black pepper, and mix with your fingers. Cut the pork into several pieces. Rub the spice mixture all over the pork.

In a large nonstick pan (or right in the pressure cooker pot, as we did it), brown the pork for about 3 minutes on each side, until the outsides are golden brown. Remove the meat and set aside.

Put the cider, water, ketchup, and liquid smoke in the pressure cooker, stir together, and simmer for 1 minute. Add the pork to the juices. Cover the pressure cooker, lock the seal, and bring to high pressure. When high pressure is reached, reduce the heat to medium-low or low. Cook for 45 minutes, adjusting the heat to maintain pressure as necessary.

Remove the pot from the heat and let rest about 15 minutes while the pressure inside the cooker comes down. Remove the pork and place in a large bowl or dish. Skim the fat off the cooking juices, and then simmer in the pot for another 5 to 10 minutes, until reduced to a rich sauce. Pour or ladle the sauce over the meat. Shred with two forks into bite-size pieces for sandwiches.

Heat the vegetable oil in a small saucepan and fry the shallots until crispy. Remove them from the oil with a slotted spoon and drain on a paper-towel-lined plate. Set aside the scallions and the shallots for garnish.

Toast the rolls. Spread barbecue sauce on rolls if desired (or you can use some leftover juice from the pressure cooker) and heap on the pork. Top with fried shallots and chopped scallions. Makes 6 to 8 sandwiches.

PULLED PORK GYROS WITH RED CABBAGE, ROASTED TOMATOES, AND CILANTRO

I took leftover pulled pork and piled it into a pita with roasted tomato and cilantro. This sandwich was a play on Greek gyros.

1 cup pulled pork (page 266)
4 to 5 medium tomatoes (I prefer yellow tomatoes)
2 tablespoons olive oil
1 teaspoon paprika
3 tablespoons Greek yogurt
1 teaspoon cumin
½ teaspoon black pepper
juice of ½ lemon
2 cups chopped red cabbage
1 pita
2 tablespoons chopped fresh cilantro

For the pulled pork: Follow the recipe for Pressure Cooker Pulled Pork Sandwich. Omit adding additional barbecue sauce at the end.

Blanch the tomatoes: Have ready a large bowl about half full of ice cubes. Score the skin of each tomato on the bottom with a cross. In a large saucepan, boil enough water to submerge the tomatoes. When the water is boiling, drop in the tomatoes and cook for about 45 seconds, until you see the skins beginning to peel away. Remove the tomatoes with a slotted spoon and immediately place them in the bowl of ice. Once the tomatoes are cool, peel the skins off.

Roast the tomatoes: Preheat the oven to 400 degrees. Place the peeled tomatoes in a shallow baking dish. Drizzle with the olive oil and paprika and stir or toss with your hands to coat the tomatoes. Roast for about 30 minutes, until slightly charred and squishy. Remove from the oven and set aside.

In a large bowl, mix the Greek yogurt, cumin, black pepper, and lemon juice. Combine thoroughly, then stir in the red cabbage.

Lightly toast the pita and slice it open. On the bottom half, lay the cabbage, pulled pork, and roasted tomatoes. Sprinkle with cilantro. Top with the other half of the pita. Hold together with toothpicks if needed. Makes 1 sandwich.

TWENTY-FIVE

> DAD: Get them sandwiches going.

> ME: I know, I'm falling behind.

> DAD: Get 'er done so you can move on to the next stage of your life.

"When do you think you'll be done with the sandwiches?" asked everyone everywhere around sandwich #250.

It was a fair question. According to my pace I would be done by June. Or, as it was suggested by just about everyone who wasn't about to be my fiancé, I could crank up the pace and do three or four sandwiches a day. "Then you'll get the ring!" "Then you can plan a wedding!" "Then you won't have to cook anymore!"

In order to bump up production, I tried to be clever and make a bunch of sandwiches in a row.

Something special had to be done for sandwich #250. I heard about an "alphabet sandwich"—a sandwich made up of ingredients representing all of the letters of the alphabet stacked between two pieces of bread—making the rounds on food blogs. I liked the idea, but I wanted to do a vegetarian version.

It took me five days to get this sandwich together.

I went to the grocery store several times, always forgetting one or two letters' worth of ingredients. Then, some vegetables didn't qualify—how was I going to get a food that started with X? (According to the all-knowing Internet, there was one vegetable that started with X: xylocarp, or coconut. So I cooked some of my vegetables in coconut oil. That was close enough.)

In the days leading up to my final execution of the Vegetarian Alphabet Sandwich, I watched several rounds of vegetables grow limp and soggy in my crisper. Between replacing vegetables and loaves of bread, by the end of this weeklong recipe construction, I must have made a dozen trips to the market. On day five I started early, making the sandwich before work while E showered and got dressed. It took two hours, possibly because I was multitasking my own morning routine of sending off emails to publicists and editors, ironing my clothes, and cleaning the kitchen between each layer of perfectly cooked vegetables.

E and I had been on rocky ground since my Bridezilla breakdown. This morning was no different; we were fighting about music.

"Is this *Whitesnake*?" I snarled. I couldn't totally hear the song coming from the office but it didn't matter. I was annoyed I hadn't picked it.

It was Pink Floyd, by the way.

Somehow, I had a sandwich ready and packed in Tupperware for E to take for lunch by the time we left for work. I then schemed on the other four sandwiches I planned to make so I could add to my count quickly.

I ate a piece of toast with apricot jam and chugged a glass of water before flying out the door with E toward the subway. As we got on the subway car and the doors closed behind us, something felt amiss.

My chest had this weird pain on the left side. I couldn't take a deep breath without a sharp jab. The pain got worse as the F train pulled out of the station. Then I felt nauseous, my stomach doing flip-flops as the train weaved through tunnels and skipped over uneven spots in the tracks. Maybe my breakfast of toast and jam and a handful of almonds wasn't enough for my commute.

As we were approaching Second Avenue, one stop away from E's office but several stops from mine, everything turned gray and blurry. "Are you okay?" E asked again.

"No. I need to sit down."

Just as the train rolled into the station, the doors opened, and hurried commuters spilled out onto the train platform, leaving empty seats. "Here, sit down," E said as he guided me toward one. But as I moved, everything went blurry again, and my peripheral vision disappeared.

"No." I pushed E aside. "We have to get off."

Sweaty and shaky, I fought through the remaining people still trying to get on the train, and threw myself onto the platform. I couldn't breathe; the stabbing pains in my chest had constricted my breathing to a shallow pant. I couldn't see in front of me more than a few paces. I somehow grabbed E before my vision turned completely black and rattled off my symptoms, so he knew, in case I couldn't tell paramedics if or when they needed to come.

"Let's get you outside to some fresh air," he said, and helped me up the stairs. I walked with my head down, only able to see my feet move up and down. I could see light ahead, but couldn't make out people's faces or backs of heads. We climbed out to the street, and I found a seat on an abandoned fire hydrant on Houston Street.

My breathing was slightly better when fresh air from outside hit my lungs. But my stomach was still queasy, and my vision blurry when I held my head up. A street vendor selling pretzels and Snapples had set up his cart a few steps behind me. I fished two dollars from my wallet and reached out to E. "Can you get me a juice?" I whined.

We popped into the nearest walk-in clinic—luckily in New York they're like Starbucks, one on every corner. The doctor asked me if I was under stress lately. I thought about it a second. "I'm always under stress," I told him. "No more so than normal." I didn't go into the whole I'm-stressed-out-because-my-boyfriend-told-me-he-would-propose-when-I-made-him-300-sandwiches-so-I'm-trying-to-make-them-as-fast-as-possible thing. Modern medicine did not have a remedy for that level of crazy.

"Try to take it easy the next few days," the doc said. "Ease off on the running and slow down a bit. And for today, try to eat five small meals," he recommended. He did not specify if those meals had to be sandwiches.

I probably should have eaten a bigger breakfast. And not run around doing fifty things before my morning commute. Sitting down for a cup of tea with E on our patio, talking to him about his upcoming day at the office, or an upcoming vacation, would have been more productive, and allotted us more quality time than the mutterings we exchanged while I was in the kitchen making a sandwich.

This is what I get for trying to manipulate fate, for trying to "speed up the sandwich making." As much as I tried to control it, again, I had to learn to just love the process.

Saturday was a better day. The sun was shining, warming the streets of Brooklyn to 65 degrees. I went for a run outside, a leisurely three-mile jog, and stocked up on spring vegetables and fruit for a hearty breakfast. I called my mother.

She sounded down, distant. She answered every inquiry of mine with mostly monosyllables. "How is Dad?" I asked.

"I don't know," she said.

"Is something wrong?"

"I don't want to get into it."

"Mom, please. I have to know. I have to keep up with his condition."

"I don't want to ruin your good day," she said, though my good day was not good as long as my father was ill and my mother depressed.

"Should I hop a plane tomorrow? I can."

"I always told you to come when I needed you. And there will come a day when I do, when it will be the day. But now, I don't know what's going to happen."

"Mom, that's the problem. We don't know what's going to happen, and I feel guilty every day I'm not there."

"Your father is so proud of you and loves watching you do your work. He wants nothing more than to see that."

I choked up. I felt like someone was holding my neck underwater. "What if I run out of time?"

My mother tried to soothe me. "We can't control time, honey. We can't control what's going to happen. Listen, you call every day, you tell him you love him. What more can you do? He'll need you when he feels bad, not when he feels good. He was good for a long time. Three years we've been dealing with this! In that time doctors have said things and given prognoses and not one of them stuck."

I feel like I wasted so much time. Five months had gone by since we were told that chemo wasn't working. Sure, we'd tried experimental treatments. We *tried*. But they weren't working. Meanwhile, in that same five months, E and I could have been engaged. Or gotten married. We could have had a wedding. Would we have had a wedding if I weren't making the sandwiches?

How many more sandwiches would my dad live to see?

I brought up the idea of a mock wedding again to my mother. The only thing he and my mother could make time for were doctor's appointments. "Dad just wants you two to be happy. That's all he needs. He doesn't need a wedding. He just wants to know you'll be happy," she said.

"Isn't that all the more reason to have some sort of celebration?" I asked.

My mother sighed. "All I know is you've been a good daughter to him, you did all you could while you were here. I have done all I can. But sometimes, I don't know, it's just . . ."

She took a pause, and then said what she shouldn't have, but what both she and I were both really feeling: "I just want the suffering to be over."

sandwich #250

THE VEGETARIAN—
A-TO-Z ALPHABET SANDWICH

Sandwich #250 had to be special. Over the top. I saw this on the blog DudeFoods.com, where the guy used a food for every letter on his A-to-Z sandwich. There are a hundred creations you could try, but I did this one with all veggies.

Avocado (¼ avocado, sliced)
Beet (1 beet, boiled, peeled, and sliced thin)
Cucumber (¼ cucumber, sliced thin)
Dates (2 dates, sliced thin)
Eggplant (2 slices roasted eggplant)
Fennel (1 bulb, sliced very thin)
Green bell pepper (½ pepper, sliced into small strips)
Horseradish (½ teaspoon)
Iceberg lettuce (2 leaves)
Jelly (½ teaspoon strawberry jelly)
Kale (¼ cup, chopped and sautéed in coconut oil—see below)
Lemon juice (½ teaspoon, sprinkled on fennel)
Mustard (¼ teaspoon)
Nuts (crushed)
Orange rind (¼ teaspoon, chopped, sprinkled on fennel)
Parsley (¼ teaspoon, chopped)
Quinoa (1 teaspoon, cooked)
Radishes (2 radishes, sliced thin)
Scallion (½ scallion, chopped)

Tomato (½ tomato, sliced)
Upland cress (1 tablespoon, chopped)
Vidalia onion (2 slices)
Watercress (1 tablespoon)
Xylocarp (1 teaspoon coconut oil to sauté kale)
Yam (½ yam, boiled, peeled, and sliced thin)
Zucchini (4 slices)
2 slices wheat bread

Toast the bread. Spread horseradish, jelly, and mustard on the bread. Stack veggies on top, any way they can possibly fit between 2 slices of bread. Cut in half. Makes 1 sandwich.

EGG-CELLENT BREAKFAST EATS

After studying the greats—Gordon Ramsay, Eric Ripert—E developed a method of scrambling eggs that I then used for several sandwiches throughout the 300.

SCRAMBLED EGGS FOR TWO

6 eggs
2 tablespoons butter
1 to 2 tablespoons heavy cream or crème fraîche (or additional 1 tablespoon butter)
handful (about ⅓ cup) chopped fresh chives
salt and pepper

Crack the eggs into a small pan on medium heat, along with the butter. Turn the heat to low. Mix the eggs and butter vigorously with a spatula, breaking down the eggs until eggs and butter are combined. Remove from heat when just combined, continuing to stir constantly, and then alternate between 30 seconds off the heat and 30 seconds on the heat until the eggs firm to the desired consistency. (For E, that is similar to risotto.) Once eggs are almost at the desired consistency, push eggs to one side of the pan and warm the heavy cream, crème fraîche, or butter in the other side of the pan. Once warm, stir to combine, and add chives, salt, and pepper. Stir a few more times, and serve.

Now, take those eggs, and use them as the base for the five egg sandwiches that follow:

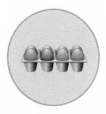

sandwich

#18

EARLY RISE—EGG AND AVOCADO SANDWICH

I thought sliced fresh avocado would be delicious on an egg sandwich. Instead, I found out that raw avocado was to be added to E's Forbidden Foods list. It's a consistency thing, E argues. He's missing out on a treasure of life—fresh scrambled egg with avocado is one of my favorite breakfast sandwiches.

5 eggs (see page 279 for scrambled egg recipe)
¼ cup chopped fresh chives
1 teaspoon chopped fresh parsley
salt and pepper
2 English muffins, halved
2 tablespoons unsalted butter
½ ripe avocado, sliced
Tabasco or other hot sauce

Start the scrambled eggs. Use the chive-and-parsley mix in place of the chives in the basic egg recipe; add them once the eggs are halfway cooked. Season with salt and pepper.

Toast the English muffins. Spread the butter on the bottom halves. Lay avocado slices and spoon warm scrambled eggs on top. Sprinkle with Tabasco sauce. Finish with the muffin tops. Makes 2 sandwiches.

sandwich

#67

IN THE DOGHOUSE—
SCRAMBLED EGG, SMOKED SALMON, AND CHIVES

Smoked salmon is one of E's breakfast staples, but it's on my Forbidden Foods list. I made this for him after I was forty-five minutes late for dinner one night, leaving enough time for a girl at the bar to make eyes at my boyfriend. Lesson learned—always be on time, or another woman will be.

6 eggs (see scrambled egg recipe on page 279)
salt and pepper
3 tablespoons chopped fresh chives
2 English muffins, halved
2 or 3 tablespoons cream cheese
4 or 5 slices smoked salmon

Make the scrambled eggs. After cooking, remove from heat and scoop the eggs out of the pan into a bowl to stop the cooking process. Sprinkle with salt, pepper, and chives and set aside. Toast the English muffins. Spread cream cheese on both sides. On the bottom halves of the muffins, lay a few slices of salmon, then scoop some scrambled egg on top. Finish with the muffin tops. Makes 2 sandwiches.

sandwich

#90

BEACH BODY—
SCRAMBLED EGG-WHITE SANDWICH WITH PEPPERS

This is a great sandwich to have before or after a workout, which E and I had to keep up with in between 300 decadent sandwiches. How did E stay so slim while eating all that meat and cheese? CrossFit workouts.

2 tablespoons olive oil
¼ cup chopped green bell pepper
¼ cup chopped red bell pepper
6 egg whites
salt and pepper
1 tablespoon dried oregano
2 tablespoons chopped fresh parsley
2 small pitas or English muffins, halved
2 tablespoons shredded mozzarella cheese
1 tablespoon Tabasco sauce (optional)

Warm the olive oil in a large nonstick pan. Cook the green and red peppers in the pan for about 3 minutes, to soften. In a small bowl, mix the egg whites with salt, pepper, and oregano and whisk with a fork. Add the eggs to the pan and scramble. Add parsley when eggs are nearly cooked. Remove from heat.

Toast English muffins or pita. Sprinkle mozzarella on the bottom pieces. Spoon the egg white and pepper scramble onto the cheesy bread. Sprinkle with Tabasco sauce if desired. Top with top piece of bread. Makes 2 sandwiches.

STEPHANIE SMITH

sandwich

#129

TOMATO, MOZZARELLA,
AND SCRAMBLED EGG BREAKFAST SANDWICH

*Take a Caprese salad. Add scrambled eggs, pile it all on an English muffin.
You've got breakfast. E and I ate this one on our balcony, where we grow our
own basil and herbs in small planters.*

4 eggs (see scrambled egg recipe on page 279)
2 English muffins, halved
1 tablespoon unsalted butter
4 to 6 slices fresh mozzarella
1 medium tomato, sliced*
6 to 8 whole basil leaves
salt and pepper

Make the scrambled eggs. After cooking, remove from heat.

Toast the English muffins. Slather butter on both sides. On the bottom
muffin halves, stack mozzarella, tomato, basil leaves, and warm scrambled
egg. Season with salt and pepper. Finish with the muffin tops. Makes 2 sandwiches.

*Naturally, I omitted the tomato for E.

sandwich

#228

CANDIED BACON, SCRAMBLED EGG, AND PARMESAN BREAKFAST SANDWICH

You will make candied bacon, and then you will eat all of the candied bacon before you can get it on a sandwich. And then you will make another batch of bacon and actually get it on the sandwich. No one will judge you.

5 or 6 slices candied bacon (see page 209)
5 eggs (see scrambled egg recipe on page 279)
1½ tablespoons grated Parmesan cheese
1 generous tablespoon chopped fresh chives
2 English muffins, cut in half
1 cup chopped greens
1 teaspoon balsamic vinegar or olive oil

Make the candied bacon. Make the scrambled eggs. Add Parmesan and chives when eggs are almost cooked. After cooking, remove from heat.

Toast the English muffins. Dress the greens with olive oil or balsamic vinegar. On the bottom muffin halves, stack bacon, greens, and scrambled egg. Finish with the muffin tops. Makes 2 sandwiches.

TWENTY-SIX

Hi Stephanie!

Love your blog. My friends told me about it with the caption "this is the worst thing we've ever witnessed in Internet history" and I actually took some time to read it. And you guys are awesome. You're demented like any proper couple should be, but still awesome. I particularly loved your chicken parmesan slow-cooker recipe. =)

Anyway, my husband had a fabulous idea for E's proposal . . . 300 engagement rings! It's only fair, right? And you could wear whichever one you wanted each day. Think of the possibilities!

Tell him he better start saving up!

—Letter from a reader

I didn't want to go to Barbados.

E had arranged a vacation for us and four friends at the beginning of May. He flew down a week before I did, to do some kitesurfing with his best friend, Graham, and set up our hotels and activities before the rest of the group arrived. I was due to join E in Barbados after I went home to see my parents for Mother's Day.

When I arrived in Michigan, Dad hugged me at the door. We sat in his office. Sitting up in a chair for longer than a half-hour sitcom was too uncomfortable since he had no muscles left to cushion his body from the seat. He lay down, grabbing his head with both bony, wrinkly hands. Those hands used to be so swollen, his wedding ring hadn't been able to fit over his knuckle at one point. Now the ring sat in a jewelry box on my mother's armoire, too big for his ring finger.

And yet, he still had a smile for me when I got home, and before I could pour myself a glass of water, asked me about work: "So, what's the good gossip in Gotham?"

On Mother's Day I woke up early, so I could spend as many waking hours with my parents as possible. Dad was in his room, sipping tea and watching political pundits argue about the economy and jobs on CNN.

I had a card for Mom, but Dad was too weak to go to the store and shop for a gift. He sent me instead.

I shouldn't go to Barbados, I thought. My heart told me I shouldn't go. So did my mother. "I'd love it if you stayed an extra day or two," Mom said. When I priced out changing my airline tickets, it was cheaper for me to buy another flight from New York to Michigan a few days after I came back from Barbados. So I did.

After booking my ticket back, I went into the kitchen with my mother, where before I could take a seat, she offered me a sandwich. "How about a sloppy Joe?" she asked.

Not a Manwich-style sloppy Joe, but one popular in New Jersey, with turkey and ham, cheese, Thousand Island dressing, and coleslaw. We sat in the kitchen together as I watched her carefully stack the sandwich. "I used to eat those like crazy when your father and I were first married," she said. "A friend of ours used to own a sub shop, and he catered our wedding. These were his specialty."

As I watched her, she looked at peace. Her hands were purposeful as she smoothed on the coleslaw and formed a perfect tower of meat and cheese, then sliced it into bite-size pieces. She stepped back, satisfied with her work. After months of watching my father's health head south and hearing from doctors that little could be done to turn it around, making this sandwich was probably the first time in months when she could manipulate positive results out of something.

It was wet, gooey, salty, and, as advertised, sloppy. The combo of salty meat, wet coleslaw, and bread tasted like a backyard picnic in 1982. The comfort of that sandwich, as well as hugs and kisses from my parents, eased my mind as I flew home to New York, repacked my bag, and headed to the airport. "I'll see you in two weeks, Dad," I told him.

He smiled.

Our Barbados vacation was not to be a romantic lovers' escape, but rather a kitesurfing boot camp, where beginners like me would take lessons and the more experienced would do long downwinders along the sandy golden beach until sunset.

Two other friends of ours, Vicky and Brad, and another buddy of Graham's, Tony, met us on the island, and the six of us stayed in a private residence on the beach. The house had a name, Joias, but no address, according to the website for the home.

E picked me up outside the airport in a Big Bird–yellow go-cart called a Mini Moke, an open-roofed car with no doors and four seats with seat belts, perfect for towing around surfboards and kite gear. It had a trunk in the back to store groceries or spare towels, and a small glove compartment where E had stashed a hip flask of rum "for the road."

He poured me a roadie—a small shot of rum on ice—knowing I would be on edge after an emotional weekend home. I sipped it while he drove on the left side of the road , weaving around curves as the wind whipped our hair around and the warm Caribbean sun bore down on our shoulders.

We pulled into a gated estate that looked like something out of a Bond movie—a large mahogany gate parted to reveal lush foliage surrounding a long two-story home. On the wall was a large crest that explained the home's grandeur—it was the former consulate of

Uruguay, and large enough for entertaining several diplomats at once. Fourteen-foot-high mahogany doors led into the great room. Our bedroom, the master, was in the corner of the second floor and could pass for a luxury apartment in New York. A king-size bed sat in the middle, leaving enough room around it for a dresser, a couch, a wall-length closet, and enough floor space for four yoga mats. The bathroom had a shower large enough for all six of us to shower at the same time under the dinner plate–size showerhead.

The first night in, we grilled fresh-cut mahimahi on our patio, and toasted the gathering with wine, rum, music, and dinner overlooking the ocean. E passed out at 9:30, right as the gang were deep in conversation about what to plan for the next day's events.

The next day, I posted this on 300 Sandwiches as my welcome to Barbados post:

I'm finally reunited with E, aka Mr. 300 Sandwiches, in Barbados!

We're here for a week of kitesurfing and relaxation with several of our friends. E spearheaded the whole trip, yet again knocking it out of the park by picking a fabulous home on the beach for us to stay in and setting up car rentals, stocking the refrigerator, and seeking out the good local restaurants all before I arrived. If there's anything the man can do right, it's vacation.

But there's one thing he doesn't do: surprises. People keep asking if we're getting married here. "No," E told me. Okay, so no surprise wedding here. And I doubt there's an engagement ring tucked inside his sandy kitesurfing bag packed with kites, ropes, board shorts, and sunscreen. My parents still hold out hope he'll surprise me with a ring this week. I think he's concentrating more on the wind than on a proposal.

I folded up the computer and made breakfast for the group: arepas with scrambled eggs, tomatoes, and onions.

"This is sandwich number two hundred fifty-six," E said.

"I can count this one?"

"Yeah, it can count towards the three hundred," E said.

Vicky, the only other girl on the trip, wanted to take me for manicures at the spa. "I just really need one," she said. I agreed.

"We should dress for the night because the boys have planned a nice dinner afterwards," she said.

I had thought I'd make fish sandwiches for dinner.

"All right, help me figure out what to wear."

I went upstairs and flipped through the shorts and tank tops I'd hung in the closet, looking for something beachy but not too formal. I grabbed the new jeweled swimsuit cover-up I'd received as a Christmas gift, and some black shorts to wear underneath. "Will this work?" I asked Vicky.

"Oooh, pretty! Yes, do that."

I pulled on my clothes, but left the flip-flops on. We were coming back home before dinner, so I could just change out of my flip-flops into wedges then.

Vicky grabbed the keys and drove us to the spa, meandering down the main drag of Barbados' south coast. We arrived at the Accuqa Hotel in about thirty minutes, ready for some spa treatment.

The waitstaff greeted us in the lobby, handed us our robes, and directed us to the warm Jacuzzi baths in the back of the resort. "Enjoy," they said, offering juice and tea. I waited for all of ten seconds before I went in on the whole E-not-proposing-in-Barbados thing.

"I can't rush the man. But I did have a total freak-out the other day," I explained while we were in the Jacuzzi. "He'll do it when he feels like it."

"True," Vicky said. "You just gotta let it happen."

The technician came in and grabbed us for manicures. I had an injury to my right ring finger that I was worried about aggravating further, so I declined. "Actually, is it possible that I can have a pedicure instead?" I asked.

"Sure, no problem," the manicurist said.

The manicurist set us up next to each other so we could continue our conversation as we got pampered. "Maybe they'll have some color or something you can do yourself for your fingers," she suggested.

"Yeah, perhaps." I shrugged. "Or maybe I'll keep them bare. They're just going to be abused by the sand and surf. Might as well wait until after we get back to New York."

I realized as my feet were being massaged by another woman that not once did I think about what the boys were doing. I assumed they tried to sneak in a kitesurfing session while we were gone.

Vicky fished through her makeup bag and started applying her makeup for the night. "This will be the first time that I've put on makeup in days," she said. "Have you tried this mascara from Maybelline? It's great." Was she implying I should put on makeup? I thought lip gloss would do. Still, I rimmed my lids with eyeliner and blotted on a bit of bronzer so I looked somewhat decent for all of the photos the gang were likely to take at dinner.

When our nails were dry, Vicky texted the boys to tell them we were en route. I was happy in the moment, cruising down the Barbadian highway, whizzing past fish cutter stands, strip malls, and pastel-colored houses.

We pulled into our private drive, and the Mini Moke was parked differently than it had been when we left. I walked in ahead of Vicky around the back of the house, but E came running out from the gazebo toward me, dressed in khakis and a soft gray T-shirt. He'd shaved and showered. He grabbed me.

"Hey there!" I said, startled.

He kissed me. Hard on the lips, holding my arms with both of his hands. After lingering on my lips for what seemed like long enough for a thirty-second commercial to air, he said, "Come here."

E grabbed my hand and hurriedly walked me over to the pool, which was lined with luminaria around the perimeter. To the right, on the mahogany deck, was a huge heart laid out in rose petals. E turned to me and grabbed my hand.

I was stunned. "What is . . . oh my . . ."

I realized it was happening. Everything. Was. Happening.

Right.

Now.

"I found something while spearfishing today," E said, standing, then bending down, then on one knee. He reached for a large clamshell sitting at the pointy end of the heart, and removed the lid. I couldn't see what was inside, because my eyes were blurry from crying and wiping away tears.

E held my right hand in his palm tenderly.

It was all coming together. Our lives, this night, our future, our pasts. Somehow, through a pool of tears, I finally found his eyes with mine.

"Will you marry me?"

When I heard those words, a flash of what my life was about to become went through my mind. More laughter. More coffees on our patio overlooking our herb garden. More runny eggs for breakfast. More holidays together with our blended families. More tickle fights in bed before we fell asleep. More adventures. More battles over who played better morning music. More time spent on Caribbean islands kitesurfing, snorkeling, scuba diving, parasailing, grilling dinner parties for our friends. All of the things we'd done many weekends before that we would do for years to come.

"Well? What's the answer?" E said as he tried slipping the ring on my finger.

I sobbed and collapsed in his arms. "Oh my God. Oh my God, yes."

The ring was sitting in the clamshell on a bed of sand, and E let go of me long enough to grab my left ring finger and slide the ring onto it. It was a tight fit, and I didn't look down to see what the ring looked like until it got stuck at my knucklebone.

"C'mon!" we both said, until finally it slid over the skin into place on the base of my ring finger—the same octagonal ring I went gaga for at Ahee's in December. It was perfect.

I grabbed E again and just wailed.

"You are the most thoughtful, loving man with a beautiful heart," I gasped between tears. "I can't wait to spend my life with you."

And then I sat in that embrace, not hearing anything but my own sobbing and his breath and the ocean for a minute.

"SHE SAID YES!" E cried out toward the house, still holding me.

"Whoooooooooo!" our friends cried out from various corners of the house, stationed to take photos from many angles to capture the special moment.

"Champagne for everyone!" Graham cried, with two glasses in hand and a bottle of Veuve Clicquot. I had spotted that bottle in the wine refrigerator yesterday, while I was putting away the wine we bought at the grocery store. Brad had hurriedly taken the bottle away from me, volunteering to organize the wine himself. Now I knew why.

Our friends gathered around for a group hug and to take a crap-ton of photos. Which I really appreciated because I can't remember much from that day.

I was breathless. My mind was spinning.

"We have to call my parents," I told E.

I danced around the pool looking for my purse, which I'd dropped on the pool deck when I finally comprehended E was proposing, and fished out my phone. I pressed the entry for Mom and Dad in my contacts list, disregarding whatever the charge was for making an international call on my phone. . . . I'd deal with that when I got the bill.

"Mom, get on Skype. It's important."

"What?" she snapped.

"Yes, do it now. And get Dad."

"Do I have to?"

"Yes, you have to! Now!"

She acted as if I were interrupting her during a board meeting. "This better be good," she said. "Give me five minutes."

I ran upstairs to our second-floor bedroom to grab my laptop, my eyes still glassy from crying and my chest fluttering from the high of the moment. I brought the computer down to the kitchen table on our patio, overlooking the ocean, and dialed my mother on Skype.

I stood out on the open-air deck with E behind me and saw my mother in the screen.

"Where's Dad?" I asked.

"He's right here."

Dad poked his drawn face into the screen. The bandage on his neck contrasted with his blue shirt and dark skin.

"Hi, Dad! I have news for you!"

Then, I put my left hand up to the laptop camera.

My father looked, and then looked closer and looked some more.

Then my mother looked. "Is that a . . . wait . . . are you . . . is that a ring? OH MY GOD!!! WHOOOOO!!! I can't believe it! Are you engaged!? WHHHHHAAATTTTT!! Oh, I can't believe it!"

My father threw a thumbs-up in the air, and then reached for a tissue and wiped his eyes, while my mother squealed in the background. E grabbed me and kissed me, holding me in a long embrace in front of the camera.

Over my shoulder, I looked at my father in the screen, smiling, his thumb still in the air, still holding a tissue with the other hand, standing alone in the screen because my mother was jumping up and down in the kitchen, frantically looking for her own tissue. My dad's eyes crinkled upward. I could see all of his teeth smiling back at me, just like when I caught that twenty-pound catfish when I was four years old in our backyard. He was, for that minute of that night, happy.

"I can't believe it! Oh my God! Let me see! OH MY GOD!" my mother was still shouting.

She disappeared out of the screen, but her voice was audible from the background.

"I can't believe it! How did he do it?"

I went through the entire story, holding up the computer over the pool to show the lanterns lighting up the perimeter, and the flowered heart on the deck. I felt like I was recounting how I had been asked to the prom, but on a much bigger, more poignant scale. "And then he asked me!" I finished.

E came up closer to speak with them via Skype. "Congratulations, Eric! You did good! I'm so happy!" my mother yelled.

"Thank you," E said. "But you guys actually knew about this before she did. I tried to tell you last week."

Unbeknownst to my parents and me, E tried to tip my parents off to the engagement the week before. Having seen my father's condition when I arrived home last week, I told E I didn't think it was fair for me to come to Barbados knowing he was still in the States sick. In response, E sent a photo of himself holding the engagement ring to my father in a private message on Facebook. But my father didn't receive it. Perhaps because I had arrived in Michigan on a Saturday and occupied my father's time so much that he never had a chance to check his voice-mail or Facebook messages.

Once E didn't hear back from my dad, he sent a text to my mother, saying he was thinking about her, and asked her to tell Dad to check his Facebook messages. They still didn't get the message.

But now, the message was clear. We were engaged.

I didn't make the fish sandwich that night. We went out for dinner, and celebrated over dinner at a large restaurant overlooking the western coast of Barbados. The next day, for lunch, I made the fish-killer sandwich, named after my dad. It was the first meal I made for E as my fiancé.

THE "MOTHER KNOWS BEST" SLOPPY JOE

My mother was friends with a guy who owned a sub shop in New Jersey called Delicatessen. He catered my parents' wedding. My mother made a sloppy Joe packed with meat and fatty condiments and coleslaw. Mighty good sandwich for game day or a summer barbecue, if you ask me.

3 slices rye bread
1 tablespoon mayonnaise
1 tablespoon Thousand Island dressing
6 slices turkey
6 slices ham
4 slices Swiss cheese
2 tablespoons coleslaw

On one side of the slices of bread, spread the mayonnaise and Thousand Island dressing. Stack half the slices of turkey, ham, and Swiss cheese. Top with 1 tablespoon of coleslaw. Stack a piece of bread. Stack more slices of turkey, ham, and Swiss cheese. Top with 1 tablespoon of coleslaw. Finish with the top piece of bread. Cut in quarters to serve. Makes 1 sandwich.

AT-HOME SNACK—
FRIED BANANA-STRAWBERRY SHORTCAKES

I treated my mom to something nice for Mother's Day. She came up with the idea of fried bananas, so I used them as the base for strawberry shortcake sammies. They're small, finger-food-size, so you don't have to feel guilty about eating more than one.

1 egg
2 tablespoons sugar
pinch of salt
pinch of baking soda
½ cup milk
½ teaspoon vanilla extract
just under ⅔ cup flour
vegetable oil, for frying
2 bananas, sliced
1 cup strawberries, halved
8 teaspoons whipped cream
confectioners' sugar, for sprinkling over shortcakes as garnish

In a small bowl, mix the egg, sugar, salt, and baking soda. Add ¼ cup of milk and the vanilla, and slowly add the flour. Add the remaining milk and combine until the mixture has the consistency of cake batter.

Heat the oil to a high temperature in a nonstick pan over medium heat. Prepare a paper-towel-lined plate or baking rack. With a slotted spoon or fork, dip the bananas in batter and coat them completely. Fry the banana slices in oil for about a minute on each side, until brown. Remove from oil and let cool on paper-towel-lined plate or baking rack.

Start with banana on the bottom, stack a few slices of strawberry, then dollop on a teaspoon of whipped cream, and top with another banana slice. Pierce with a toothpick to hold together, and sprinkle with confectioners' sugar. Serve warm. Makes at least 8 shortcake sandwiches.

sandwich

#257

THE FISHKILLER—FISH CUTTERS

Who knew it would take only 257 sandwiches to get him to pop the question? Totally went against my plan. For one, I'd never even heard of a fish cutter until we came to Barbados. It's their national sandwich, made with fried flying fish, tartar sauce, and some hot Bajan pepper sauce. I made my own version for our official engagement sandwich, and named it after my father, since he was the original "Fishkiller." Check his Facebook page. That's his nickname.

1 pound mahimahi, cut into sandwich-sized steaks about
¼ pound each
1 teaspoon cumin
1 teaspoon black pepper
1 teaspoon seasoned salt
2 to 3 tablespoons olive oil
mango salsa (see recipe below)
4 salt bread buns (or round Kaiser or sub rolls)
lettuce (optional)
relish (optional)
½ teaspoon Bajan or other hot pepper sauce (be careful!)

Mango salsa
1 mango, diced
1 tablespoon lime juice
1 tomato, diced

2 tablespoons chopped fresh cilantro
salt and pepper, to taste

Season the fish with cumin, black pepper, and seasoned salt. (I'll be honest: I used what I found in the cupboard at the house. If it's good mahimahi, you won't need a lot of seasoning.) Brush olive oil on both sides of the fish. Grill about 4 minutes on each side, flipping once, until cooked through (the fish will be opaque, not translucent, throughout). Remove from the grill.

In a small bowl, toss together the mango, lime juice, tomato, cilantro, salt, and black pepper until thoroughly combined.

Slice the buns in half (but not all the way through) and stack with the mango salsa, mahimahi, lettuce, and relish if using, and a sprinkle of Bajan hot pepper sauce—it's spicy, so use caution. Close the buns. Serve with rum or a side of fries. Makes 4 sandwiches.

TWENTY-SEVEN

As I flew back from Barbados on that mid-afternoon flight to JFK—where the stewardesses cooed, "Congratulations, Stephanie and Eric, sitting in seats 7A and 7B, on their engagement!" to all two hundred passengers on board over the PA system—all I could think about was whether or not Dad would make it to our wedding, now that a wedding was definitely happening. "You'll get to walk me down the aisle," I texted him.

When I landed, I called Mom to ask about when we should schedule the wedding.

"Why rush?" she said.

"Um, for obvious reasons."

"Listen," she said, pausing for maximum I-am-telling-you-what-the-deal-is-and-there-is-no-debating-me effect. "We want you to enjoy your time of being engaged," she said. "I want you to just spend this time together, and take your time planning. And your father feels the same."

"But," I said, pausing, "can't we do something to celebrate with him while we can? At least an engagement gathering?"

My mother sighed. "I'll bring it up to him. But really, there's no sense in making any plans. We just don't know what's going to happen."

After a series of phone calls and some light arm-twisting, we made plans to have a Father's Day/engagement party with my family and E's parents at my parents' Michigan home. Father's Day was about a month away. We wouldn't have vows, but we'd have cake, champagne, decorations, and fun music, so at least Dad would enjoy one of the parties around our wedding, even if, God forbid, he didn't make it to the actual ceremony.

I flew home to Michigan for Memorial Day weekend. I told E to stay behind and come on Father's Day, since it was just three weeks later. I could see my father standing on the patio, watching me as I pulled the car into the driveway and shifted into park. He stood upright, but looked even thinner than he had just a few weeks prior.

Dad held the door open and meandered toward me, hugging me, then grabbed my left hand and stuck it in front of his face. He mouthed "Oh!" and gave me a thumbs-up. "E did good," he whispered. "Real good."

For the next two days, Dad and I sat in silence, watching television, exchanging looks between us as if we both knew these treasured moments would be scarce in the coming months. We watched our Sunday-morning news programs in his office, decorated with photos of him decked in camouflage hunting gear and flannel shirts, a wood armoire that held some of his shooting gear, stacks of boating magazines and catalogues for Cabela's and L.L.Bean. We shared sections of the Sunday papers—the *Chicago Tribune,* the *Kalamazoo Gazette,* and *The New York Times*—passing them back and forth as we finished, and leaving the advertisements out for Mom, who grabbed them and sat with us between cooking and doing the laundry.

Later that afternoon, as the sun started to fall lower in the sky, Dad lay down on the couch in his office, his pain-stricken body looking for a comfortable spot in the stillness while he closed his eyes. I peeked in on him to see if he needed anything, then turned away when I saw him sleeping. He cleared his throat to get my attention. Then, he waved me inside.

I stood next to him. "Do you need something, Dad? Water? Juice?"

He shook his head, then grabbed my hand and pulled me close to him. I sat next to him, and put my arm around his shoulder. He nestled into it and took a deep, soothing breath.

We stared out of the picture window in his office that looked out onto the lake in our backyard, the lake where he'd found so much enjoyment for thirty years. The lake he taught me to swim in, to fish, to find frogs in. The lake he ice-fished in during cold Michigan winters with his buddies, and where he took his wife and little girl out on sunny winter Saturdays. The lake that he'd bought property on back when he was a new father, hoping that his young daughter would appreciate the beauty of the outdoors as he did. Among the lush oak and maple trees that framed the lake, we could see the sun dancing off the surface of the water, and spotted a rabbit skipping across the path toward our dock where the pontoon sat.

He reached across his body with his right hand and grabbed my left hand, turning it over to take one last glance at my engagement ring. Then he held my hand, and closed his eyes, finding a small bit of comfort, pain-free, in that moment on the couch with me.

The next morning, I left for the airport before 5:00. My parents kissed me good-bye, both bleary-eyed in the morning light. I would return, with E, just a few weeks later for our Father's Day/engagement party.

"I'll see you in a few short weeks, Dad," I told him.

"Okay," he replied, unfazed. He kissed me on the cheek, gave me a squeeze as if I were just driving around the block, expecting to see me in a few brief moments once I'd run a few errands.

TWENTY-EIGHT

Six days later, I got a phone call from my mother.

"Your father's in the hospital. It's not looking good."

I hopped on the first flight out the next morning. E came with me. We didn't make it in time.

Six hours before I boarded a plane to Michigan, Dad slipped away with Mom by his side, holding his hand, peacefully.

"I could have made it," I told my mother. "I could have been there in time. Why wasn't I there?" In fact, there was no way I could have made it in time. One cannot outrun an aneurysm, particularly when the aneurysm has a seven-hundred-mile head start.

"You couldn't control this, Stef. No one could."

It had been two weeks since I got engaged, two weeks since my father saw my left hand with a sparkly ring flash against the computer screen. Just when I was about to start a life with the love of my life, I had to say good-bye to the man who gave me life and taught me about love.

TWENTY-NINE

At his service, a military burial befitting a United States Navy man—
"Taps," uniformed servicemen, flag presentation, gun salute—E
stood by my side, holding my hand, my shoulders, helping me stand
when I wanted to collapse into the ground. He cooked dinner for my
mother and me at the house when we were too preoccupied to think
about food, and he held me tight in bed as I cried myself to sleep.

The pastor referred to E as a member of the family, a son, "the best
son-in-law Art could have ever imagined." E sat two seats away from
my mother during the entire wake and service, close enough for her
to reach out to him when needed.

Two weeks. Dad had seen me engaged for only two weeks.

During my last visit home, I fell asleep on my father's couch in his
study while Dad sat upright watching TV in his office chair. I would
catch Dad staring at me as I slept. I wondered what he was thinking
about. His pain? What would happen to me once he was gone? Or
was he content with how I'd turned out? Was he proud of me? Was
he proud of the woman I'd become? I hope he was.

The only sense I can make out of the uncanny timing is that Dad
held on long enough to get confirmation that his little girl would be
okay. Not okay, as in taken care of—I'd always done a good job of
taking care of myself—but okay, as in settled, with a future ahead of
me with the man I wanted to be with, a man who made a promise to
my father when he asked for my dad's hand in marriage, and a man
who had made good on that promise.

Dad was there for the most magical moment, the engagement,

the one that we expected to be marked by sandwich #300, but instead came at #257, the "Fishkiller" Fish Cutter, named after him and his love of fishing. He saw the joy on my face, my smile reaching across the entire fourteen-inch computer monitor when I called home via Skype to tell my parents the news.

Days after the funeral, I looked at my engagement ring now, and couldn't find the energy to smile.

As much as I tried not to be sad, I couldn't help but be angry because he wouldn't be at my wedding. Angry that he wouldn't meet his grandchildren. Angry thinking that I could have made those damn sandwiches faster, and maybe we would be married by now, before Dad had passed on.

For days after his death, I couldn't look at anything joyful without seeing my father's face. Fluffy cumulus clouds on a summer day. French bulldogs. Boats. Ice cream sandwiches. I wondered if I'd ever be able to look at anything that made me happy without crying.

But my father, the original Fishkiller, the loudest man in the room, with a laugh that rattled the shutters, was not a man who wanted us to sit around and cry over his passing. He would want us to smile, enjoy life, feel the sunshine on our skin, and laugh about whatever was around us. He wanted us to love each other, to be happy, to be present.

Dad didn't want us to force our wedding, to rush into such an important event to accommodate him. Instead, he stepped aside, so that we could plan a wedding on our time, our terms, with worry-free minds and unlimited possibilities. He wanted us to do whatever we wanted to express how much we loved each other. Giving each other "everything in our power," like he had promised my mother on their first date.

Dad would still be with us at the wedding. Except he'd have a better seat. From above, in heaven, in the front row, healthy as can be, smiling down at us as we said "I do."

THIRTY

My eighty-seven-year-old neighbor made me laugh this morn-
ing. Somehow we got on the topic of women and marriage. He
told me at his age, he would enjoy having a good sandwich more
than being with a woman. Is that what us guys have to look
forward to when we reach that age?

—Reader comment on Facebook

The last sandwich.

What will be my swan song, the ever powerful 300th sandwich?
Will it be over-the-top, outlandish, the biggest sandwich that ever
lived?

Will I have someone else make it, like some famous chef or ca-
terer?

Or, being that I already have the ring, will I make nothing?

I knew exactly what it would be. I have known from the beginning of this adventure what I would serve E for the 300th sandwich.

It will be the very first sandwich I made him: turkey and Swiss.

But this time, it will be prepared differently. I will make the sandwich with confidence. Confidence that I know I'm doing it right.
That I know exactly how he likes his bread, how much mustard I
should use, what lettuce to layer on the bread before placing the turkey on top, layering like layers of phyllo dough.

And I will not be nervous when I present it, wondering if he will like it. E will.

I will expect, as my mother did every time she made my father a sandwich, to only get an empty plate scattered with a few crumbs in return, the only remnants of the satisfactory meal.

And then? I'll make another one. And another one. And another.

After we got engaged, I heard from many readers who shared their stories of love and food, recipes for awesome sandwiches, and advice and suggestions on wedding planning. I now had friends in Kentucky, London, and Bangalore. Through sandwiches, I'd built a deeper relationship with E, and new relationships with thousands of strangers. I forged a closer relationship with my *Post* colleagues not only because my love story became one of the biggest viral phenomena of 2013, but also because I brought in samples of my sandwich creations from time to time.

That's right, I was still working—working harder than ever. And blogging, and cooking, and running, and pole dancing, and traveling, and doing whatever else I felt like doing after E proposed.

I had not thrown away my career and identity for an engagement right and sandwiches. Contrary to the chirpings of the social media peanut gallery, the feminist movement was still intact after the 300 Sandwiches movement.

A wise reader of 300 Sandwiches wrote to me after I detailed the challenge of deciding on the last few sandwiches on the site:

You'll never be finished. I mean, technically you'll reach 300 and be done with the "challenge," and if he proposes, great. But just because you got the ring doesn't mean you should stop making an effort and making delicious sandwiches.

—Leah V.

When you're in a relationship with someone you love—yourself, your mate, your parents—you never stop "making the sandwiches."

As in, you never stop doing the things that make them happy. You never stop opening doors for your girlfriend, or kissing her on the cheek, or bringing home her favorite flavor of ice cream. Or at least, you shouldn't.

Because these small things, these repetitive nice gestures, are what keep the other person coming back. They're what make them happy you're in the room. They're a reminder that you love someone.

Marriage is about knowing—and fulfilling—your partner's wants and desires. After thirty-eight years of marriage, my mother knew how to make my father a sandwich, so to speak. After two years of dating, I was still getting to know E. His likes, dislikes, turn-ons, passions—and how he takes his turkey sandwich.

I remember how timid I was to make E's first turkey and Swiss sandwich. It took me ten minutes to decide whether or not to toast the bread. I worried if I'd used the right mustard and if he'd approve of my condiment-to-filling ratio. But he devoured it, and asked for 299 more. After that, my confidence grew with each sandwich I made.

I hope after decades together, I have the same swagger in making sandwiches as my mother.

I'll never stop making the sandwiches. And E won't stop "making the sandwiches" for me. That is, he will still make me coffee in the morning, and bring it to me on the patio so we can have some quality time together before we leave for work.

He still makes me smile when I want to cry, and he still finds something positive to say even in the darkest of situations. He still does what he says he's going to do, from taking us on snowboarding vacations to showing up for dinner on time.

He also still manages the kitchen for most of our dinner parties.

He also surprises me. Turns out I'm the one who didn't do surprises. Hence my need to always control things. I've learned to let that go. Somewhat.

.   .   .

"What should we cook tonight?" E asked. It's Tuesday. Or Thursday. Or any night we're home. We are cooking. Together. For each other.

"What are you in the mood for?"

"Hmm," he said, his eyes trailing upward to the ceiling as he pulled me tighter. "Fish," he says.

"Halibut, with tomatoes and that pesto sauce you like?"

"Uh-huh. Good idea."

We parked the car and grabbed a cart; meandering through the aisles, tossing in fresh vegetables, cheese, and bread, and all of the other little ingredients needed for our dinner. E lingered over the smoked salmon at the deli counter, while I went back to the vegetable section and picked up kale. I gave up kale for 300 sandwiches because it was on E's Forbidden Foods list. Now, and forever, I'm going to eat what I damn well please on my own damn sandwich, thank you very much.

We picked up our necessities, including bread, mayonnaise, Greek yogurt, and chocolate chips, paid for our groceries at the checkout counter, and headed for the car.

E pushed the cart while I fished the car keys out of my purse with my left hand. My engagement ring sparkled in the sunlight as I pulled out the keys, a ring that took six months to construct. I smiled as I unlocked the trunk and watched E unload the groceries.

In the kitchen, E and I quickly unloaded the groceries together, then laid out everything we'd need for dinner. We danced around each other as we shuffled from the refrigerator to the oven to the sink. I chopped onions like a pro and tossed them into a bowl, while he sautéed meat. "Should I pop the tomatoes in the oven to roast?" I asked him.

"Yep, and I'll get started on the fish," he said. We opened a bottle of crisp rosé as we cooked, and poured two glasses. E raised his glass to mine. Clink! "To us," he said. "I love you."

We cranked up some music, the soothing voice of Diana Krall wafting from our speakers from E's dinner party playlist, comprised of the many tracks his father had shared with him. The sizzle of fish and vegetables was slightly louder than the jazz piano from Krall's cover of Frank Sinatra's "Fly Me to the Moon." "*In other words, I love you,*" the sultry voice sang as I pulled the tomatoes out of the oven, and E took the fish off the heat.

We plated dinner together, him swiping a dab of jalapeño cilantro emulsion on the plate before I placed the fish and topped it with a heaping spoonful of roasted tomatoes. "That looks good," he said. I winked at him.

We sat at our oversize farm table together, the same table where we'd hosted Thanksgiving dinner together for a dozen of our friends, the table where I'd scoured through recipes for sandwich ideas and directions for a properly prepared steak. The farm table that was currently decorated with an etched silver tray and tea set from E's grandmother Sharon, two issues of *Martha Stewart Weddings,* and a vase full of hydrangeas.

Across from the table was a bookshelf stocked with books, including a whole shelf of cookbooks by Eric Ripert, Momofuku, *Gourmet* magazine, and one called *The Flavor Bible,* which had the most stains on the pages by far, because either E or I referenced it before just about every meal we made. A photo of E's parents together on a boat, holding E when he was no more than four years old, sat on the bookshelf facing us. Next to it, a photo of my parents on one of their first dates, my mother wearing a long salmon-colored maxi dress, my father in a suit and sporting a freshly trimmed Afro. Though E's parents were white and mine were black, both of our fathers had the same Burt Reynolds mustaches on their upper lip, like every dignified Reagan-era executive.

On the wall facing the table were the heads of two antelopes shot by my father, and on the opposite wall was the deer E's grandfather shot, which had hung on the wall of his old apartment. The three stuffed animals looked down at E and me, it seemed, with a protective eye. Keeping watch on their young offspring as they ate, staving off threats from the outdoors.

I stole a glance at E after I took a bite. He reached over and kissed me on the cheek. "Fish is good, right?"

I took a sip of wine, sat on the couch, and smiled at E from behind while he hunched over his plate to shovel in his last bit of fish and roasted tomatoes.

"Indeed," I said.

THE MRS. E—
TURKEY AND SWISS ON TOASTED COUNTRY WHEAT

The sandwich that started it all—except with more confidence and love than before. I know exactly how much turkey to use, what greens he prefers, and how brown he likes his bread toasted. This is how I will make E's turkey and Swiss for the rest of our days. Or at least until he puts Swiss cheese on the Forbidden Foods list.

2 slices nutty wheat bread
1½ tablespoons whole-grain Dijon mustard
4 leaves romaine lettuce
6 slices smoked turkey (enough to pile up to about ¾ inch thick)
4 slices Gruyère cheese
black pepper

Toast bread until crunchy, but not so stiff that it can't absorb the mustard. Spread Dijon mustard on both slices of bread. Blot dry the lettuce, trim the leaves to fit, and place on both slices. Fold the smoked turkey slices on top of the lettuce. Add the cheese slices. Sprinkle with black pepper. Put the two sides of the sandwich together and smush down gently. Cut on the diagonal and serve with dill pickles and tortilla chips. Makes 1 sandwich.

ACKNOWLEDGMENTS

There are many people for whom I would make a sandwich.

First, Mom and Dad. Mom has made me many sandwiches since I've been alive. She also encouraged every crazy idea I've ever had, including one to make my boyfriend 300 sandwiches, launch a blog, and write a book about it. She read every page, sometimes twice, and gave me constructive criticism. Mom, I love you. Don't ever forget that.

Dad, I hope you're looking down from heaven and are proud of what you've left behind. I miss you every day.

To my publishers at Zinc Ink, David Zinczenko and Steve Perrine, who wanted to make my crazy story into a book back when I'd only made about 52 sandwiches. To Michael Freidson and Kimberly Miller, who fine-tuned drafts of my prose over summer weekends and provided words of encouragement when I was my most insane. I'm especially appreciative to Kimberly for tackling this job a few weeks before her own wedding. I appreciate your guidance and patience with little me.

To my agents at William Morris Endeavor, Jason Hodes, Andy McNicol, Jenni Levine, and Bradley Singer, who believed in the potential of *300 Sandwiches*. Thank you for telling me to come back in a year after our first meeting, and opening the door when I returned.

To Stephanie Jones, for listening, advising, making me laugh, brainstorming, and being a dear friend.

To Graham Milton, who not only was the first person who told us, over margaritas, that 300 sandwiches for an engagement ring was a great premise for a blog, but also helped to design our logo, tasted many a sandwich on a Sunday night, and snapped our engagement photos in Barbados. You have been such a dear friend to E, and now, to me. Thank you.

To everyone at the *New York Post,* including editor in chief Col Allan and president Jesse Angelo, who supported me and encouraged me to keep making those sandwiches. Special shout out to features editor Margi Conklin, who allowed E and me to tell our story in her section, and celebrated every life event with us as we moved towards marriage. To Page Six editor Emily Smith, for always supporting me during sandwich making and the book, and to deputy editor Ian Mohr, my dear friend. You're like the older brother I never had. Thank you.

To my friends and family who made me laugh when I was in the thick of writing, and reminded me that I could accomplish anything. Even making a sandwich.

For Renee and William, my in-laws, who never expected their family to be exposed to the media because of their son's girlfriend. Thank you for playing along and supporting me, even when news reporters were stalking you at your house looking for information on when and how your son was going to propose to the "sandwich girl."

And finally, for Eric, for without you, there would be no us. Or sandwiches. I love you, forever and always.

ABOUT THE AUTHOR

Stephanie Smith is a journalist, author, and founder of the food and romance blog 300sandwiches.com. She is a senior reporter for the *New York Post,* and has written for *Women's Wear Daily, Money, Mediaweek, Vibe, People,* and *Playboy.* A Chicago native and graduate of Medill School of Journalism at Northwestern University, Stephanie resides in Brooklyn, New York, with her soon-to-be husband, Eric.

ABOUT THE TYPE

This book was set in Minion, a 1990 Adobe Originals typeface by Robert Slimbach (b. 1956). Minion is inspired by classical, old-style typefaces of the late Renaissance, a period of elegant, beautiful, and highly readable type designs. Created primarily for text setting, Minion combines the aesthetic and functional qualities that make text type highly readable with the versatility of digital technology.